The Blair identity

Manchester University Press

The Blair identity

Leadership and foreign policy

Stephen Benedict Dyson

Manchester University Press
Manchester and New York
distributed in the United States exclusively by Palgrave Macmillan

Copyright © Stephen Benedict Dyson 2009

The right of Stephen Benedict Dyson to be identified as the author of this work
has been asserted by him in accordance with the Copyright, Designs and Patents
Act 1988.

Published by Manchester University Press
Oxford Road, Manchester M13 9NR, UK
and Room 400, 175 Fifth Avenue, New York, NY 10010, USA
www.manchesteruniversitypress.co.uk

Distributed exclusively in the USA by
Palgrave Macmillan, 175 Fifth Avenue, New York,
NY 10010, USA

Distributed exclusively in Canada by
UBC Press, University of British Columbia, 2029 West Mall
Vancouver, BC, Canada V6T 1Z2

British Library Cataloguing-in-Publication Data
A catalogue record for this book is available from the British Library

Library of Congress Cataloging-in-Publication Data applied for

ISBN 978 0 7190 7999 3 *hardback*

First published 2009

18 17 16 15 14 13 12 11 10 09   10 9 8 7 6 5 4 3 2 1

The publisher has no responsibility for the persistence or accuracy of URLs for external
or any third-party internet websites referred to in this book, and does not gurantee
that any content on such websites is, or will remain, accurate or appropriate.

Typeset by Helen Skelton, Brighton, UK
Printed in Great Britain
by CPI Antony Rowe, Chippenham, Wiltshire

Contents

List of tables

1 Blair's wars

Secluded in his private Downing Street study and facing the most fateful decisions of his political career, Prime Minister Tony Blair conferred with his 'inner-circle', a group of close advisers upon whom he relied heavily. John Scarlett, head of the Joint Intelligence Committee, had just returned from briefings in Washington and shared with the group his discoveries: US military action against the Saddam Hussein regime in Iraq was, to all intents and purposes, 'inevitable'. Should Britain be a part of this coming war, which was sure to be both risky and controversial? Jack Straw, the Foreign Secretary and close Blair ally, felt that the case against Saddam was 'thin'. He was 'not threatening his neighbours, and his WMD (weapons of mass destruction) capability was less than that of Libya, North Korea or Iran'. The Attorney General, Lord Goldsmith, told Blair that under international law the US proposition was a dubious one, as 'the desire for regime change was not a legal basis for military action'.[1]

Yet Blair had made up his mind. He had given a commitment to US president George W. Bush that the British would support him, and so his thoughts were focused on how to sell the war domestically and internationally. He saw Saddam Hussein as 'evil', felt that there was little chance of resolving the matter through United Nations weapons inspections, and believed that he could replicate his previous foreign policy successes, especially in Kosovo and the immediate aftermath of September 11 2001, in influencing the United States and the broader international community. In the weeks following this meeting, as rumours of its content swept the government, Blair was approached by senior Cabinet colleagues and asked to schedule a full official discussion of Iraq policy. Blair rebuffed these requests point blank, stating, not entirely accurately, that any decisions on Iraq were far in the future.

This was characteristic of Blair's style. He was comfortable with making decisions based on fundamental principles, and intolerant of ambiguity and complexity. He preferred to operate through informal groups of hand-picked advisers, disdaining formal bodies like the cabinet and bureaucracies like the Foreign Office as 'stuffy' and cumbersome. The scope and ambition of Iraq policy was characteristic of a consistently proactive, interventionist foreign policy strategy. Finally, the belief that he could be simultaneously influential with the Americans, persuasive to the international community, and convincing to the British public was a hallmark of Blair's confidence in his own efficacy. Indeed, the central argument of this book is that British foreign policy has been decisively shaped by this worldview and leadership style of Tony Blair during his time in office. Simply put, I argue that a convincing explanation of British foreign policy from 1997 to 2007 must take full account of the personality of Tony Blair.

To trace and evaluate the impact of Blair on British foreign policy and international affairs obviously requires careful analysis of the events involved. With this as a goal, I augment the available documentary record with focused interviews with senior politicians, diplomats, and military figures: those who worked with Blair during this period. Across the major events of Blair's 1997–2007 tenure, I seek to answer three crucial questions:

- What was Blair's foreign policy style and worldview?
- What difference did the Blair style make to British foreign policy choices during this period?
- What difference did Blair make to the outcome of events and the policies of others, especially the United States?

Tony Blair and British foreign policy

The irony of making an extended argument about the significance of Tony Blair in international politics is that Blair entered office focused almost entirely upon domestic affairs and with little foreign policy experience. Clare Short, who served in a key foreign policy post as Secretary of State for International Development, recalls that 'when we were in opposition, he never to my knowledge ever expressed a view on anything to do with foreign policy'.[2] Indeed, prior to taking office,

Blair, with a modernizing domestic agenda, had expressed a desire to spend as little time as possible on the 'outside world'.[3] General Charles Guthrie, who as Chief of the Defence Staff from 1997–2001 was the most senior military officer in the UK, recalls that there was a concern about Blair's national security credentials prior to his election: 'We must do something about the Labour Party', was the feeling among the military establishment. 'They know nothing about defence whatsoever. We have to try and educate them.'[4] This concern prompted Blair's communications director, the mercurial Peter Mandelson, to suggest that the major unanswered question about the putative prime minister was, in an unwitting gift to future chroniclers of his deeds, 'will TB fight wars?'[5] Immediately after taking office Blair himself suggested that the answer was perhaps not: 'Mine is the first generation', he said, 'able to contemplate living our entire lives without going to war, or sending our troops into battle'[6] – an incredible statement to reflect upon now.

Blair, of course, quickly discovered that he had very strong foreign policy convictions and a liking for the world stage. General Guthrie found that Blair picked up the taste for international affairs quite readily: 'He listened, he was a quick learner, and he realized that once he was prime minister, the British ... had a unique role. We were alongside the Americans, and had armed forces that were prepared to fight.'[7] Far from never sending the troops into battle, he committed forces to conflict five times in his first six years, becoming the 'waringest' prime minister in British history. He quickly developed a highly interventionist foreign policy doctrine, underpinned by a worldview of black and white clarity, and enacted through tightly held policy processes. This style and modus operandi, solidified in the 1999 Kosovo intervention and finding further expression in Sierra Leone, Afghanistan and Iraq, is the consistent theme running through British foreign policy in Blair's decade in office.

My argument is that this policy and leadership posture is the outward manifestation of the key elements of Blair's political personality. By systematically analysing every answer Blair has given to a foreign policy question over the last ten years in the British House of Commons, I build a portrait of his worldview and style grounded in solid empiricism. I use methods designed to take the words of politicians as indicative of the way they think about the world, not by naively taking their assertions at face value, but rather by systematically searching their verbal output for key words that have been shown to be linked to stable underlying dispositions. In particular, I show that in

relation to other world leaders and British prime ministers, Blair measures as significantly higher in his *belief in ability to control events*, an
aspect of leadership style linked to proactive, ambitious policies and a
feeling of efficacy in relation to international issues and actors. Blair
measures lower in *conceptual complexity*, a key dimension of cognitive
style that shapes how much differentiation individuals see in the world
around them, with Blair's lower score disposing him toward very clear-
cut, unequivocal framings of issues and actors. Finally, Blair is moti-
vated by a high *need for power*, an aspect of leadership style focused
upon the personal control an individual asserts over decision-making
processes, and their collegiality and inclusiveness, or lack thereof.

These measurements of Blair's traits – a high belief in the ability to
control events, a low conceptual complexity, and a high need for power
– in effect act as hypotheses concerning his behaviour in international
politics and decision-making style. They are tested against, and where
supported act as an explanation for, Blair's actions in the key events of
his tenure: the Kosovo war of 1999 and the Sierra Leone intervention
that soon followed, the response to 9/11 and the war in Afghanistan,
and, seminally, the invasion of Iraq in 2003 and the aftermath of that
war. Together, these episodes tell the story of Tony Blair's impact on
British foreign policy.

In Kosovo, Blair was the most hawkish NATO leader on the use of
force, arguing strongly for continuing the air campaign against Serbia
even when it seemed to be accelerating the ethnic cleansing that it was
designed to halt, and pushing hard for the introduction of ground
troops. His belief in the necessity of this was such that he found himself
in conflict with his close ally President Clinton. Blair defined very
broad policy goals, promising not only to prevent the Serbian military
from exercising its will upon Kosovo but also to secure the return of
the Kosovar refugees to their homes. He viewed Milosevic as simply a
brutal dictator, and his ethnic cleansing policies as evils the like of
which had not been seen in Europe since the Second World War. No
compromise deal with him could possibly be contemplated. Blair
acquired during the Kosovo intervention a strong preference for
making policy in small, informal groups, and avoiding regular, bureaucratized channels. He took a huge risk in committing himself to ambitious policy goals when success was far from certain and in defiance of
the advice of many colleagues and officials. Counselled by some to
consider a compromise with the recalcitrant dictator – and thereby
follow a well-established pattern of British and NATO policy in earlier
Balkan crises – Blair refused out of hand.

He gained great confidence in his foreign policy style and world-view during the Kosovo intervention, confidence reflected in his statement, at the height of the conflict, of a broad and ambitious grand strategy: the 'Doctrine of the International Community'. Here Blair, in the midst of fighting a humanitarian war the outcome of which was highly uncertain, chose in effect to 'double-down' by setting out an agenda for intervention around the world on grounds of both security and humanitarianism, and arguing, in effect, for the overturning of the post-Westphalian system of international relations. His new doctrine was given an early test in the West African nation of Sierra Leone, where warlordism and brutality were rife. When several British soldiers were taken hostage, Blair did not hesitate to launch what was a very dangerous rescue mission, and agreed also to British forces remaining in country to bolster international peacekeepers, an action that changed the dynamics of the situation and provided a crucial measure of stability.

With his stature as a world figure established following Kosovo, Blair sought to continue the close alliance he had built with President Clinton with the new US leader, George W. Bush. September 11 2001 set in motion a sequence of events that would define Blair's foreign policy legacy. His response to 9/11 was rooted in his fundamental foreign policy style. He instinctively cast the conflict in Manichean terms of good and evil, a fundamental battle between terrorists, their state sponsors, and the civilized world. As with Milosevic there could be no compromise with terrorism, which had to be defeated in all its manifestations. Blair perceived that 9/11, by focusing attention on the security problems of the twenty-first century, represented an opportunity to deal not only with terrorist violence, but also its underlying causes. In particular Blair considered that the plight of the Palestinians was the root cause of many of the Middle East's problems, and that a comprehensive response to 9/11 must include progress on this issue. Characteristically, he thought he could fundamentally shape the US response to the events of 9/11, ensuring that it was proportionate and well-considered.

However, Blair's policy was again perhaps overly ambitious. The US accepted his help diplomatically, but kept the UK at arms length in Afghanistan and was reluctant to accept his counsel to multilateralise the counter-terrorism campaign. Similarly, Blair's attempts to build an international coalition in active support of the United States ran up against concern, in the UK and elsewhere, about the increasingly belligerent tone emanating from Washington. Crucially during this period, Blair missed the significance of two post-9/11 shifts within the Bush administration – the declining influence of Colin Powell coupled with the increasing power of secretary of defense Donald Rumsfeld and vice president Dick Cheney, and the decisive acceptance within the administration, and by the president, of the tenets of what had become known as 'neoconservatism'.

The former development shifted influence over policy away from Powell's State Department: a section of the US government instinctively in tune with Blair's aims and with which he and his ministers had formed a strong relationship. Instead, Rumsfeld and Cheney, increasingly in the ascendance, saw Blair as a potentially useful spokesman but as someone who also represented a multilateralism they found distasteful. The increasing rise of neoconservative principles was also not fully appreciated by Blair, who operated on the assumption that arguments about coalition building, working through the United Nations, and engaging in renewed efforts on Israel-Palestine were winnable – a position that represented a basic misunderstanding of the ideology of neoconservatism.

The decisions Blair made in this period set him upon a course that would culminate in the Iraq war. When attention within the Bush administration began to shift to Iraq, Blair was quick to offer support for the basic principle that something should be done about the Hussein regime. His black-and-white framing of the world, and belief in the efficacy of an activist posture, did create a basic sympathy toward many of the arguments the administration made about the threat from Saddam and the unpleasant character of his regime. Further, Blair recognized perhaps more quickly than colleagues, both cabinet and continental, that if the Bush administration was determined to go to war then there was little anyone could do to prevent them from doing so.

Elements of his policy made good sense, but in other ways he fell foul of his over-confidence in his ability to shape events. In particular, he over-estimated his ability to shape the circumstances under which the war would be fought, and ended up committing forces without the support of the international community and the United Nations. Moreover, his ability to shape the policies of the Bush administration was less than he seems to have supposed – the US approached the UN in a hostile fashion which seemed almost guaranteed to prevent the emergence of consensus, and Blair's continued efforts to push for a resolution of Israel-Palestine were given little more than lip-service. Finally, Blair radically over-estimated his abilities to shape the domestic picture in the UK, and found himself leading a deeply sceptical nation into war.

This ensured that the Iraq intervention was seen as a hugely personal war for Blair. The prime minister was in an exposed position, and he desperately hoped that the decisions would be vindicated both by discovery of extensive weapons of mass destruction programmes and the creation of a stable, democratic postwar Iraq. Of course, neither of these developments came to pass, and the recriminations have been severe. The whiff of duplicity over the presentation of WMD intelligence has dogged the prime minister, but of much more lasting significance was the degeneration of Iraq into vicious insurgency and near civil war. Blair was hugely frustrated by the handling of the occupation, but lacked the influence with the Americans to compel them to change course, and was unwilling to break with them in public.

Linking these events has been the style of Blair – proactive and confident of his personal efficacy, clear cut and moralistic in his framing of issues, and directive and controlling in his decision making. It is a distinctive combination, one that led to early success in Kosovo and Sierra Leone, but calamitous failure in Iraq.

The book

I seek in the following chapters to detail and document the basic case made above. In the next chapter, I elaborate a theoretical approach to the foreign policy of states that bridges levels of analysis, and show how concerns of power, threat, and strategy mandated by the international environment are mediated through and defined by issues of personality, perception, and belief at the individual level of analysis. In short: individuals matter in international relations. This general theory of foreign policy is made relevant to our specific concerns through a consideration of the US-UK alliance, and the imperatives that bear upon British prime ministers, who lead a principal junior partner of the global hegemon in a unipolar international system. Readers less concerned with the place of the argument within international relations theory can skim this chapter without fatally prejudicing understanding of the broader consideration of Tony Blair and his time in power.

In Chapter 3, I provide systematic evidence for the claims made about Blair's personality and its distinctiveness in relation to other British prime ministers and other world leaders. I introduce content analysis procedures by which Blair's personality traits are measured, and draw specific hypotheses about the behaviours to which they are linked. Again, some readers, satisfied by the portrait of the Blair style presented above, can move to the chapters on Blair's role in the major foreign policy events of his decade in office with minimal loss of understanding.

In Chapters 4, 5, 6 and 7, I explore in depth the impact of Blair on the seminal events of Kosovo and Sierra Leone, 9/11, the invasion of Iraq and the postwar situation. In each case, I seek to account for Blair's behaviour and British foreign policy first by considering the *actor-general* factors of power and threat emphasized in traditional international relations theory. I then show how the Blair style was crucial in each episode in understanding what happened. Finally, for each episode, I assess the difference Blair as an individual made to British foreign policy and to the ultimate outcome in wider terms.

In Chapter 8, I consider the implications of Blair and this study of him. What judgments can we ultimately make about his influence and his foreign policy? What does an individual as unique as Blair tell us about international relations? I conclude that, in real-world terms, Blair's style made a key difference to British foreign policy in each of the crucial episodes under consideration. Britain would not have been as forward leaning in Kosovo and Sierra Leone, would not have outlined such ambitious goals in the 'war on terror', and would have been much more cautious toward, and perhaps ultimately resiled from, the Iraq intervention, had someone else been leading the country. The incentives and constraints of alliance with the world's superpower, and the security challenges of rogue states and international terrorism, would have been faced by any British prime minister during this period, but *actor-specific* theory leads us to the conclusion that Blair played a determinate role in these key episodes. In international relations, the case of Tony Blair makes the point in vivid fashion that *individuals matter*.

Notes

1 Memorandum from Matthew Rycroft to Sir David Manning, *Iraq: Prime Minister's Meeting*, 6/23/2002. Available at www.timesonline.co.uk/newspaper/0,,176-1593607,00.htm, accessed 2 May 2005.
2 Author interview with Clare Short, by telephone, 30 April 2007.
3 Dennis Kavanagh, 'The Blair premiership', p. 14, in Anthony Seldon and Dennis Kavanagh (eds), *The Blair Effect 2001–5* (Cambridge: Cambridge University Press, 2005).

4 Author interview with Lord Guthrie, by telephone, 20 June 2007.
5 John Kampfner, *Blair's Wars* (London: Free Press, 2004), p. 9.
6 Tony Blair speech in Paris, 27 May 1997. Available at www.number 10.gov.uk/output/Page1022.asp, accessed 7 February 2007.
7 Author interview with Lord Guthrie, 20 June 2007.

2 Neoclassical realism and leader psychology: a theory of foreign policy

'As a professor', recalled Henry Kissinger after having completed careers in both academia and in government, 'I tended to think of history as run by impersonal forces. But when you see it in practice, you see the differences personalities make.'[1] I argue in this chapter that Kissinger the professor and Kissinger the statesmen were both correct: 'impersonal forces' and 'personalities' combine and interact in any compelling explanation of foreign policy choices. Such explanations, while beginning with the international system, must end with the political leader, conceptualized as an autonomous individual with distinctive beliefs, goals, and motivations that decisively shape their choices.

Power considerations are an important 'first cut' at explaining foreign policy, but must be combined with an understanding of the goals, perceptions, and decision style of political leaders to provide convincing analyses. While those primarily interested in what happened and why during the Blair era can skip this discussion without becoming hopelessly lost, it would be unfortunate if those concerned with over-arching issues of explanation in international politics did so. This is to say that my aim is not solely to provide a narrative account of some interesting decisions made by a particular figure during a certain period of time, but rather to explain the specific case of Blair's actions through the development of more general principles concerning why things happen in international affairs.

The theory of foreign policy I outline in this chapter has three major components:

1 States are constrained and compelled by power considerations in an anarchical international system. All goals of state foreign policy –

seeking security, increasing one's influence and spreading one's values – ultimately require material power in order to be successfully realised.

2 Power considerations are indeterminate causes of foreign policy behaviour. Unit-level factors mediate between systemic imperatives and foreign policy actions.

3 The most significant unit-level factor is the decision maker – the political leader as an individual – whose goals and worldview can decisively shape state action.

With these principles as a starting point, I show that a combination of new work within the realist paradigm and established research within the foreign policy analysis subfield can be joined into a convincing account of foreign policy. I also begin to indicate how the theory can be applied to the British context with a focus upon the power considerations activated by the alliance with the United States – the hegemon in a unipolar, anarchic international system.

Neoclassical realism and foreign policy

A necessary starting point in explaining a state's foreign policy is to recognize that the state is concerned about its survival and security, and pursues these goals through the acquisition of power: the development of military capacities and the formation of alliances. The anarchic international environment and the frequency of conflict provide strong imperatives to gear foreign policy behaviour toward these goals. The distribution of power across the units in a system creates distinctive constraints and incentives that bear heavily upon a state. The state, socialized into this environment, will often behave in accordance with the logic of the situation, and if it does not, is subject to punishment in terms of diminished security. This is the logic of neorealism, the dominant theoretical perspective in international relations for nearly thirty years.[2] The logic is powerful, compelling, and a source of great insight into recurrent patterns of behaviour at an aggregate level such as war, balancing, and alliances.

It is also a profoundly under-determined account of the foreign policy of a given state in a given situation. With the sole system-level variable in play, several different and sometimes entirely opposite foreign policy responses are logically deducible from the same situational circumstances.[3] It is therefore no real surprise that the historical record is replete with states facing similar situations from a neorealist standpoint, yet acting in entirely different ways.[4] Many contemporary international events of paramount importance, such as Soviet behaviour at the end of the cold war, are flatly inconsistent with neorealist predictions.[5] This, coupled with the repeated insistence of its chief proponent that neorealism is a theory of system-level outcomes rather than unit-level choices, and so shouldn't be used to explain foreign policies,[6] has prompted the development of a new school of realist thought that incorporates a wider range of causal variables. In terms of intellectual history, this new school returns to the complex causal tapestries of earlier realisms such as that of Thucydides and Hans Morgenthau, and has come to be termed 'neoclassical realism'.

Neoclassical realists, a group including scholars such as Jack Snyder, Randall Schweller, William Wohlforth, Jeffrey Tallifero and others, accept the system-level imperatives of anarchy within a given distribution of power as the best starting point for explaining foreign policy actions. They accept Kenneth Waltz's argument that his 'theory of international politics bears on the foreign policies of nations while claiming to explain only certain aspects of them. It can tell us what international conditions national policies have to cope with.'[7] They also agree with J. David Singer that analysis begins, rather than ends, with systemic factors, and that a useful theory of foreign policy must 'illuminate the decisional links between the environmental conditions and the behaviour of nations making up that system'.[8] Structural theories are a vital 'first cut', providing a baseline orientation in understanding a state's foreign policy, but when behaviour differs from the baseline expectations, unit-level variables must be introduced.[9] As Gideon Rose puts it:

> [Neoclassical realism's] adherents argue that the scope and ambition of a country's foreign policy is driven first and foremost by its place in the international system and specifically by its relative material power capabilities. This is why they are realist. They argue further, however, that the impact of such power capabilities on foreign policy is indirect and complex, because systemic pressure must be translated through intervening variables at the unit level. This is why they are neoclassical.[10]

One of the more significant of the unit-level variables is the individual political leader. Some structural realisms had conceived of individual decision makers as essentially rational actors that non-problematically perceived and responded to environmental imperatives, and could therefore be regarded as human embodiments of the 'state' acting in its own best interest.[11] For Waltz, the rationality of decision making was not an iron-law of his structural realism, yet irrationality carried such heavy costs that leaders who acted contrary to systemic imperatives would soon be replaced and their policy courses corrected.[12] However, the rationality assumption is not a necessary part of realism, except in the most basic sense that policy makers do things for some reason.[13] Indeed, as George points out, 'to describe behaviour as "rational" is to say little more than that the actor attempts to choose a course of action that he hopes or expects to further his values' – whatever they may be.[14]

In fact, the perceptions and goals of decision makers can vary when faced with the same objective structural situation – a point that was central to the first major amendment of Waltz's neorealist theory: Stephen Walt's argument that states balance not against power, but against *perceived* threat.[15] This argument, which takes account of the fact that 'flesh-and-blood officials actually make foreign policy',[16] has been central to many neoclassical realist advances.[17] As Friedberg concludes: 'Even if one acknowledges that structures exist and are important, there is still the question of how statesmen grasp their contours from the inside, so to speak, of whether, and if so how, they are able to determine where they stand in terms of relative national power at any given point in history.'[18]

The individual decision maker, whose behaviour is conditioned but not determined by environmental conditions, should thus be central to neoclassical realism. The incorporation of first-image, individual-level variables allows for more precise explanatory accounts of state foreign policy, and allows neoclassical realists to move away from the mechanistic and under-determined behavioural predictions which had created so many empirical anomalies in the structural realist research programme. Yet, incorporating individual-level variables within a wider realist framework carries two formidable challenges. The first is methodological – how can we 'get inside the heads' of statesmen to understand their goals and perceptions? This is the central question of Chapter 3, where I introduce a method for systematically measuring the individual characteristics of decision makers.

The second challenge is theoretical: how can individual-level variables be incorporated in a progressive, rather than an ad hoc manner? The constant danger in adding variables to an existing research programme is that the move is essentially defensive, with empirical anomalies 'solved' by the expedient of adding successive wrinkles to the framework of the theory. Thus, the theory accumulates variables that are not necessarily consistent with its initial postulates, and that move the theory away from parsimony and towards description. As this process continues, it becomes increasingly difficult to separate one theory from its competitors, and to specify empirical circumstances that the theory could *not* explain, leading eventually to a non-falsifiable, and indeed non-theoretical, research programme. The programme becomes 'degenerative' as a theoretical enterprise,[19] a charge that has recently been levelled against realism in general and neoclassical realism in particular.[20]

A neoclassical realist theory of foreign policy must be specific about *when* and *how* individuals matter, otherwise the dangers of ad hoc introduction of variables and post hoc 'sweeping under the carpet' of empirical anomalies are essentially unavoidable. Fortunately, a great deal of conceptual work has been done on these issues, largely within the fields of foreign policy analysis and political psychology.

The importance of individuals

The postulate that objective structures do not determine individual actions and therefore cannot be sufficient explanations for state behaviour has been accepted for decades in the subfield of foreign policy analysis.[21] Indeed, the founding principle of the subfield is that the agency of states, whose actions are ultimately determined by individuals, is not endogenous to structural systemic conditions.[22] More specifically, 'politics is a matter of human behaviour, and behaviour … is a function of both the *environmental situations* in which actors find themselves and the *psychological predispositions* they bring to those situations'.[23] Convincing explanations of international actions therefore must contain a well-specified theory of agency.

Individuals can make a decisive difference in three key areas of a state's foreign policy. First, individuals set the goals and objectives for the state. Is policy to be proactive or reactive? Are the state's goals primarily to achieve security for the homeland, or more ambitiously to spread the values and ideals of the state and thereby reduce the aggregate level of conflict in the system? Second, individuals can choose the means by which these goals are to be pursued. What should be the balance between military force and diplomacy? Are goals best pursued through multilateral means and as part of international institutions, or by acting alone? Third, individuals can shape the process of decision making. How inclusive should the process be? Is there a wide canvassing of views within the elite and public, and an attempt to make policy based upon consensus, or does the leader make policy based upon their perception of the national interest, with little regard for the views of others?

The key point of congruence between neoclassical realists and foreign policy analysis is that these questions can be shaped, but are ultimately not *determined*, by power considerations. The international system acts by 'significantly limiting the menu of foreign policy choices considered by a state's leaders at a particular time, rather than in forcing the selection of one particular item on that menu over another'.[24] For example, considering state goals, neoclassical realism tells us that no leader will deliberately risk their security and all leaders will want to maintain or improve their relative power position in the international system. But, beyond national survival, the goals that they want to pursue using national power will be the result of the combination of international environment, domestic context, and the individual worldview of the leader.[25] As Byman and Pollack note: 'Individuals set the ultimate and secondary intentions of a state ... Of course, a country's strategic position, domestic politics, culture, and other factors – both systemic and domestic – also shape a state's intentions, [however] individuals can often transcend these factors, play them off against one another, or otherwise exercise a direct and decisive influence on state behaviour.'[26]

A theory positing the combination of different explanatory variables must be clear about the manner in which the variables combine, and the circumstances under which their relative explanatory weight will vary. When will personalities be important? In a practical sense, individuals are important in each and every circumstance, as they represent the final decision unit. However, on many occasions environmental factors provide such strong incentives that individual beliefs and perceptions have a 'mirroring' effect – they represent obviously sensible responses to current conditions and are choices that the overwhelming majority of individuals faced with those circumstances would make. On other occasions, individual worldview and style can have a 'steering effect', directing policy in ways not determined by and even counter to the circumstances.[27] The key question, of course, is when do individuals 'mirror' and when do they 'steer'? Fred Greenstein specifies two considerations that can help us here, arguing that when two crucial conditions are satisfied, we can be confident in asserting that an individual was important to an outcome.[28]

The first condition is that of 'action dispensability'. If the actions of an individual are removed from the events to be explained, do those events still occur? If the events would occur even if the actions of the individual were removed, then we cannot give much weight to the importance of the individual in this case. However, if removal of the individual's actions would lead to a significant change in the outcome, then we are in business – the actions were 'indispensable' to the outcome. This is often a question of the strategic placement of the individual in relation to the events, and the degree of malleability within the broader environment. High-level decision makers, and especially chief executives, are much more often in a position to take event-defining actions as compared with lower-level bureaucratic functionaries. The specific choices of a president, prime minister, or dictator are more likely to be key to an outcome than those of a private in an army. The impact of strategically positioned individuals upon events is magnified when situations are ambiguous, non-routine, and require rapid decision making. These imperatives tend to remove decision making from routine organizational and bureaucratic processes, and act to concentrate power in the executive branch of governments. Therefore, ambiguous, threatening, or non-routine situations tend to increase the likelihood that the actions of individuals will be consequential. War, crises, and periods of flux in the international system thus tend to enhance the impact of prominently placed individuals.[29]

The second of Greenstein's conditions is that of 'actor dispensability'. Would any individual, faced with the same set of circumstances, have taken broadly the same actions? Again, this is a function of two factors. First, the degree to which the individual holds strong and distinctive beliefs and predispositions concerning the matter at hand. The stronger and more distinctive these are in comparison with others who could have occupied their post, the more likely that the individual will behave differently than another person in that situation. Second, the clarity of the situational imperatives is key. The classic example of unambiguous situational imperatives is that of a room on fire: one need only know that an individual is non-suicidal to predict that they will run for the exit. However, due to the inherent complexity and ambiguity of international affairs, the room may rarely appear to be on fire for decision makers, and if they think it is, it may be the product of an incendiary imagination. If the individual holds distinctive beliefs or goals compared with other possible leaders and the situation is ambiguous enough to allow some leeway in response, then we have actor 'indispensability' – the characteristics of the individual are causally necessary to their response. If *both* conditions of action and actor indispensability are satisfied, then we have a case of 'non-substitutability': the actions of an individual, as shaped by their distinctive goals, perceptions, and motivations, are necessary in explaining the outcome.[30]

From the discussion so far, two conclusions should be drawn. First, neither the environment nor the individual separately cause outcomes – it is the interaction between the two. By addressing both environment and individual through precise conceptual lenses, I hope to have made this point in a way that is coherent theoretically. Second, it should be clear by now that the logic behind judging the importance of individuals is, by necessity, counterfactual in nature.[31] Lacking experimental control, we cannot stage a re-run of the Russian revolution without Lenin, or of the 1980s with a fit Andropov in the place of Gorbachev. The tape of history runs only once, as Phillip Tetlock and Aaron Belkin aptly put it.[32] Nonetheless, we can examine the characteristics of individuals and the situations they faced, and separate out those situational imperatives that would have borne decisively upon anyone, and those areas where individual framings, decisions, and motivations made a difference. At root, we are asking two admittedly difficult questions:

1 Would any individual, faced with these circumstances, have acted in the same way?
2 If this individual had not acted as they did, what difference would it have made to the outcome?

What do we gain?

The theoretical framework developed above avoids pathologies inherent in the study of power politics absent individuals, and individuals absent power politics. Realism absent individuals, as discussed by the neoclassical school, generates indeterminate predictions and is thus unsuited to the analysis of foreign policies. A focus on individuals absent consideration of the aggregate power situation, however, can fall foul of the opposite pathology – the reductionist explanation of events by reference to ultimately spurious epiphenomena. Considerations of power are far from determinate: they are subject to perception and choice of response by individual actors, are often ambiguous, and several different strategies can be considered reasonable responses to the same circumstance. These are therefore conditions that are ripe for the influence of individuals. By the same token, individuals do not act with complete autonomy from the prevailing material situation, and attempting to explain the policies of a state, and international outcomes, purely from the standpoint of individual actors risks spuriously attributing explanatory weight to first-image variables, when choices and outcomes were effectively predetermined by structural factors. As Rose summarises: 'Realism ... is a theoretical hedgehog: it knows one big thing, that systemic forces and relative material power shape state behaviour. People who ignore this big insight will often waste their time looking at variables that are actually epiphenomenal. Yet people who cannot move beyond the system will have difficulty explaining most of what happens in international relations.'[33]

Application to British foreign policy

How does the general theory of foreign policy developed above apply to the specific case of British foreign policy under Tony Blair? This assessment, of course, is the central task of the remainder of this book. Nonetheless, we can make some preliminary observations at this point, indicating in broad terms aspects of the international environment that would have borne upon any prime minister in Blair's place.

A neoclassical realist theory compels us first to consider the distribution of power within the international system, and Britain's role within it. The leitmotif of the Blair era has been the alliance with the United States, and viewing this relationship through the realist lens of power and security is an important baseline for analysis, allowing us to understand aspects of Blair's policy even before considering him as an individual. The US-UK relationship is asymmetrical in nature, with one partner significantly more powerful than the other. This creates distinctive alliance dynamics: the ability of the senior (and inability of the junior) partner to act unilaterally, and a high degree of 'dependence' – in security, diplomatic, and economic terms – of the junior partner upon the senior.[34] The junior British partner therefore has significant interests in maintaining the alliance with the United States. Management of alliances is not straightforward, however, as Snyder notes:

> Management involves pursuing both common interests and competitive interests and this is essentially a process of bargaining, either tacit or explicit. The most fundamental common interest is to preserve the

alliance; having made the alliance in anticipation of benefits, the partners have a stake in keeping those benefits flowing. The primary competitive interest is to control or influence the ally in order to minimize one's own costs and risks. What gives rise to both these management tasks is the likelihood that allies will have at least some divergent interests or even conflicting interests. Although their common interests will have been sufficient to induce them to ally in the first place, their divergent and conflicting interests will constantly threaten to pull them apart. The job of alliance management, in a nutshell, is to counter these centrifugal tendencies.[35]

Indeed, junior allies such as the UK face two primary fears in their relationship with a senior partner. The first is the fear of abandonment – the senior ally will come to value the relationship less than the junior, and will, being much more powerful, have other alliance options, including the option to act unilaterally. If the junior ally proves difficult or disloyal or is simply no longer useful, the senior ally may withdraw the benefits of alliance. Junior allies seek to reduce the danger of abandonment by proving their utility and loyalty.[36] Paradoxically, however, these very actions increase the risk of the other danger, entrapment: 'being dragged into a conflict over an ally's interests that one does not share, or shares only partially'.[37] While the antidote to fear of abandonment is to cleave closer to the senior partner, the palliative for entrapment is to seek to restrain the ally through the threat of defection, withholding support during a specific crisis, or insisting on exercising influence over specific policies. Given that the alliance is asymmetrical, junior allies must demonstrate supreme skill in maintaining the alliance and charting a course between abandonment and entrapment. The brute fact of this alliance situation is that the junior ally has a weak hand to play when dealing with the senior partner. In considering the situation any individual in Blair's position would have faced, we must therefore be sensitive to the constraints and opportunities presented by being the leader of the junior ally of the hegemon in a unipolar system.

Stephen Walt, analysing the strategies of response to overwhelming American power available to enemies and allies, argues that the key question for a close ally like Britain is 'how can you use American power to magnify your own position on the world stage, and to help you accomplish your own foreign-policy goals?'.[39] Walt argues that Blair followed – indeed was the 'poster child' for – a strategy of 'bonding': wherein 'by cultivating a close strategic relationship with the United States – in effect, ingratiating themselves with key US leaders – foreign officials hope to gain direct influence over US policy deliberations and foreign policy initiatives'.[40] This is not a perfect strategy – the brute material facts mean the US might not play along and give anything in return for the flattering attention, and a more certain strategy is to influence US policies through penetration of the domestic political system à la Israel, but for a junior ally 'bonding' is a reasonable strategy to adopt in the face of US power.

In addition to sensitizing us to the importance of the US-UK alliance, a neoclassical realist 'first cut' reminds us of the importance of the power and threat elements of the Blair foreign policies. Kosovo, the war on terror, and the attack on Iraq each had, as we shall see, security rationales comprehensible from a realist standpoint. Blair worried, as would any leader entrusted with the security of the British state, about instability in the Balkans, the reputation of NATO, the threat of transnational terrorism, and the potential nexus of unpleasant dictators and weapons of mass destruction. He did interpret and at times exaggerate these threats in ways that, to a degree explored in the remainder of the book, was idiosyncratic, but he did not invent them, and any individual in his place would have had to make choices in response to them.

The neoclassical realist aspect of our theory therefore points to the importance of the dynamics of the US-UK alliance and the politics of threat and power projection as an explanation of British foreign policy during the Blair era, sensitizing us to the interests of a mid-sized power with a close relationship to the most powerful state in the system. Blair, and indeed anyone who was prime minister during this period, would have faced imperatives not only 'to secure some world role by ingratiating Britain with the USA, but also the necessity to (re-) insure Britain against some unknown rainy day ... and the choice of insurance company hardly needs justifying'.[41]

However, a spare materialist account is not on its own sufficient to explain Blair's policies. The activist interventionism and explicit moralism of the Blair policies, and the Manichean worldview they evidence, are not deducible from material circumstances alone. As we will see, the Kosovo intervention is hard to explain in purely realist terms, as are many aspects of the Iraq decisions. Even the response to 9/11, the episode in which a spare realist explanation gets us the farthest, is far better accounted for by the interaction of power and personality than by power alone. The theory developed above leads us to expect that Blair's worldview, rooted in his personality and individual style, would shape his perception and response to the power situation in the world. While any prime minister would want to be on good terms with the sole superpower, Blair's proactive and moralistic worldview magnifies the value of the alliance with the United States, as it offers a means to achieve goals Britain could not achieve alone. As Naughtie puts it, Blair's 'moral convictions would have meant little without the pact with the sole superpower'.[42] There is no realistic means by which a state with Britain's capacities could have dealt with Milosevic, the Taliban, or Saddam Hussein absent the power of the United States. Part of the 'alliance dependence' of the UK upon the US is that the relationship provides the potential for a significant world role for an essentially middle-ranking state. For a prime minister as activist in foreign policy as Blair, this multiplies the strictly material incentives to maintain the alliance with the United States.

Is not Blair's moralism inconsistent with realism? Not if one is clear on the difference between description and prescription.[43] Blair was not, I argue, a realist in the sense of being concerned solely with security and the balance of power – his goals were much more expansive than that. However, realism describes many of the key facts Blair faced: that to promote his values and enact his worldview, consideration of the basic material realities of the international system was necessary. The preponderance of power in the international system resided in the United States, and therefore Blair would have to be sensitive to and solicitous of his powerful ally in order to achieve his goals.

Conclusion

I have sought to indicate in this chapter that I do not intend to offer a free-wheeling narrative of Blair's actions, nor treat his decisions as if he operated in a strategic vacuum. Rather, the intention is to use what we know about general patterns of behaviour in international politics, and the place of individuals within them, to think systematically about Blair's impact on British foreign policy and on international politics. He faced some hard facts about the world that were beyond his control – the international system was dominated by a spectacularly powerful state with whom he inherited a longstanding alliance, and there were threats and opportunities within that system – characterized by anarchy, competition, and the ultimate primacy of material capacities – that he would have to deal with. In order to understand the difference Blair made as an individual, we must properly conceptualize the *actor-general* aspects of the context in which he worked. Indeed, I have sought to make a broader point in this chapter: that considering environmental factors as they shape the decision menu facing individuals with distinctive beliefs and motivations is the more promising means of investigating and explaining foreign policies in general. This does, however, raise a further tricky issue – how can we measure the individual characteristics of leaders in a reasonable way?

Notes

1 D. L. Byman and K. M. Pollack, 'Let us now praise great men: bringing the statesman back in', *International Security*, 25:4 (2001), 108.
2 K. N. Waltz, *Theory of International Politics* (New York: McGraw-Hill, 1979).
3 T. J. Christensen and J. Snyder, 'Chain gangs and passed bucks: predicting alliance patterns in multipolarity', *International Organization*, 44:2 (1990), 137–68.
4 P. Schroeder, 'Historical reality versus neorealist theory', *International Security*, 19:1 (1994), 108–48; R. Schweller, *Unanswered Threats: Political Constraints on the Balance of Power* (Princeton, NJ: Princeton University Press, 2006), p. 6.
5 R. N. Lebow and T. Risse-Kappen (eds), *International Relations Theory and the End of the Cold War* (New York: Columbia University Press, 1995).
6 K. N. Waltz, 'International politics is not foreign policy', *Security Studies*, 6:1 (1996), 54–7.
7 Waltz, *Theory of International Politics*, p. 72
8 J. D. Singer, 'System structure, decision processes, and the incidence of international war', in M. I. Midlarsky (ed.), *Handbook of War Studies* (Boston, MA: Unwin Hyman, 1989), p. 8.
9 R. L. Schweller, 'New realist research on alliances: refining, not refuting, Waltz's balancing proposition', in J A. Vasquez and C. Elman (eds), *Realism and the Balancing of Power: A New Debate* (New Jersey: Prentice Hall, 2003), p. 346.
10 G. Rose, 'Neoclassical realism and theories of foreign policy', *World Politics*, 51:1 (1998), 146
11 E.g. J. J. Mearsheimer, *The Tragedy of Great Power Politics* (New York: W.W. Norton, 2001).
12 S. Brooks, 'Dueling realisms', *International Organization*, 51:3 (1997), 454.
13 Schweller, 'New realist research', pp. 324–5.
14 A. L. George, *Presidential Decisionmaking in Foreign Policy: The Effective Use of Information and Advice* (Boulder: Westview Press, 1980), p. 67.
15 S. M. Walt, *The Origins of Alliances* (Ithaca, NY: Cornell University Press, 1987).
16 J. W. Taliferro, 'Neoclassical realism: the psychology of great power intervention', in J. Sterling-Folker (ed.), *Making Sense of International Relations Theory* (Boulder, CO: Lynne Rienner, 2006), p. 40.

17 W. Wohlforth, *The Elusive Balance: Power and Perception During the Cold War* (Ithaca, NY: Cornell University Press, 1993); Schweller, 'New realist research', p. 317; Rose, 'Neoclassical Realism', pp. 146–7.

18 A. L. Friedberg, *The Weary Titan: Britain and the Experience of Relative Decline* (Princeton, NJ: Princeton University Press, 1988), p. 8.

19 I. Lakatos, 'Falsification and the methodology of scientific research programmes', in I. Lakatos and A. Musgrave (eds), *Criticism and the Growth of Knowledge* (Cambridge: Cambridge University Press, 1970), pp. 91–106.

20 J. Legro and A. Moravscik, 'Is anybody still a realist?', *International Security*, 24:2 (1999), 5–55; J. A. Vasquez, 'The realist paradigm and degenerative versus progressive research programs', in C. Elman and J. A. Vasquez (eds), *Realism and the Balancing of Power: A New Debate* (New Jersey: Prentice Hall, 2003), p. 23–48; F. Zakaria, 'Realism and domestic politics: a review essay', *International Security*, 17:1 (1992), 177–98.

21 R. C. Snyder, H. Bruck and B. Sapin, *Foreign Policy Decision Making* (New York: Free Press, 1962); V. Hudson, *Foreign Policy Analysis: Classic and Contemporary Theory* (Lanham, MD: Rowman & Littlefield, 2005).

22 D. G. Winter, 'Personality and political behavior', in D. O. Sears, L. Huddy and R. Jervis (eds), *Oxford Handbook of Political Psychology* (New York: Oxford, 2003), p. 110.

23 F. I. Greenstein, *Personality and Politics: Problems of Evidence, Inference, and Conceptualization* (Princeton, NJ: Princeton University Press, 1987), p. 7.

24 Rose, 'Neoclassical realism', p. 147

25 S. Renning and S. Guzzini (2001), 'Realism and foreign policy analysis', Copenhagen Peace Research Institute Working Paper. Available at www.ciaonet.org/wps/rys02/index.html, accessed 1 April 2008; Shibely Telbami, 'Kenneth Waltz, neorealism, and foreign policy', *Security Studies*, 11:3 (2002), 163.

26 Byman and Pollack, 'Let us now praise', p. 134.

27 M. Schafer and S. G. Walker, 'Democratic leaders and the democratic peace: the operational codes of Tony Blair and Bill Clinton', *International Studies Quarterly*, 50:3 (2006), 561–83.

28 Greenstein, *Personality and Politics*, pp. 41–2.

29 O. R. Holsti, 'Foreign policy viewed cognitively', in R. Axelrod (ed.), *The Structure of Decision* (Princeton, NJ: Princeton University Press, 1976), pp. 18–54.

30 Greenstein, *Personality and Politics*, p. 42.

31 R. M. Merelman, 'Review of personality and politics: problems of evidence, inference, and conceptualization', *American Political Science Review*, 64:3 (1970), 919.

32 P. E. Tetlock and A. Belkin, *Counterfactual Thought Experiments in World Politics: Logical, Methodological, and Psychological Perspectives*, (Princeton, NJ: Princeton University Press, 1996).

33 Rose, 'Neoclassical realism', p. 165

34 C. A. Kupchan, 'NATO and the Persian Gulf: examining intra-alliance behavior', *International Organization*, 42:2 (1988), 324–5; A.

Goldstein, 'Discounting the free-ride: alliances and security in the post-war world', *International Organization*, 49:1 (1995), 48–9.

35 G. H. Snyder, *Alliance Politics* (New York: Cornell University Press, 1997) p. 165.

36 Snyder, *Alliance Politics*, p. 184.

37 G. H. Snyder, 'The security dilemma in alliance politics', *World Politics*, 36:4 (1984), 467.

38 Snyder, *Alliance Politics*, p. 322.

39 S. M. Walt, *Taming American Power* (New York: WW Norton, 2005), p. 16.

40 Ibid., pp. 191–2.

41 S. Azubuike, 'Still buying insurance? The realism behind Tony Blair's post-September 11th evangelization', *The Review of International Affairs*, 3:1 (2003), 71.

42 J. Naughtie, *The Accidental American: Tony Blair and the Presidency* (New York: Public Affairs, 2004), p. xvi

43 Telhami, 'Kenneth Waltz, neorealism, and foreign policy', p. 165.

3 Tony Blair's personality and leadership style

How can we understand and measure the political personality and leadership style of individuals in positions of power? While we may accept the case made in the previous chapter that individuals can and do influence political events, this does not solve the thorny problem of knowing which aspects of an individual's worldview and beliefs are significant, nor provide us with a way of measuring these putative casual variables in a systematic fashion. Indeed, the real objection to studying individuals as significant causal factors in political affairs has often seemed to be less that they are irrelevant to outcomes, as common sense and a surface-level acquaintance with history disabuses most of this notion, but more that the researcher finds herself so tangled in disputes over conceptualization and intractable measurement problems that the waters are more muddied by the attempt to study individuals than if the individual is simply assumed away.

In this chapter, I suggest we can do a little better than this. I review the commonly raised methodological objections to the study of individuals, taking full note of their gravity. I do, nonetheless, hope to show that the task of studying significant individuals can be accomplished systematically. Politicians leave thousands of clues as to their worldview and style each day, through the words they speak. Indeed, few love to talk as much as the politician. I introduce techniques through which we can measure the individual characteristics of these verbally effusive individuals through careful content analysis of the words they speak, and thereby begin to organize the chaotic and idiosyncratic nature of the human personality into more ordered categorizations that can be used to understand and predict the behaviours of prominent individuals.

In the second part of this chapter, I apply these techniques directly to Tony Blair through analysis of every answer he has given to a foreign affairs-related question in the House of Commons throughout his decade in office. I show that Blair has a distinctive style and worldview in relation to both the average world leader and his predecessors in the office of British prime minister. I check the accuracy of the portrait these techniques present of Blair against the judgments and recollections of his colleagues and biographers – finding a good fit between my data and their observations - and draw explicit hypotheses as to how we would expect a leader with Blair's style to behave in international affairs. This will complete the preliminaries and allow us in the following chapters directly to address Blair's impact on the key events of his tenure.

First, we must address some of the difficulties of the enterprise: how can we conceptualize and measure the relevant individual characteristics of political leaders in ways that are both valid and reliable?

The assessment of political leaders

Studies of the individual characteristics of political elites face a series of challenges. First, we are confronted with the basic problem of needing to understand the real motivations and well-springs of action of an individual, while only knowing that individual from a distance and through a carefully managed public image. The most direct way of understanding an individual within wider society would be to have them recline on the proverbial couch and allow a trained professional to interview them directly and at length. Unsurprisingly, prominent politicians are not particularly amenable to requests from researchers to undergo psychoanalysis and have the results made publicly known. Politicians do, of course, submit to being interviewed by journalists and this can be a useful source of insight into their worldview, but of course journalists are properly concerned with news rather than collecting systematic evidence that might bear on theory-building and testing, and politicians are of course quite good at managing the answers they give to journalists. Further, relying on being able to interview individuals, even should they submit to it, poses one obstacle that no one has yet been able to overcome: politicians are in the habit of expiring with the same frequency as the rest of the human race and, once dead, are somewhat unresponsive as interview subjects.

This lack of access has not been the only problem. It has been very difficult to agree on precisely how to conceptualize politicians as individuals – which aspects of their personality and belief system are relevant to explaining and predicting the decisions they make? One approach, until recently the most common, has been to work inductively, with the researcher seeking to immerse herself in all the knowable materials on an individual - diaries, letters, family situations, professional activities - and search for patterns of behaviour that might be indicative of underlying motivations. If the analyst is skilled and trained in psychological concepts, a convincing picture of the individual can be constructed. This approach, known as 'psycho-biography', was perhaps most successfully applied by Alexander and Juliet George in their magisterial and field-defining *Woodrow Wilson and Colonel House* – a study of the American president that detected commonalities in his response to the great challenges of his life and plausibly argued that these were outward reflections of deep-seated internal motivations, largely the result of a troubled relationship with his father.[1]

Whatever the success of the formidably skilled Georges in implementing this approach, there are good reasons to be cautious about its general applicability. Many of the problems centre on the difficulty in moving beyond single-shot studies of individuals. Operating inductively, plausible and convincing accounts of individuals can be constructed, but these accounts do not easily build upon one another, nor, often, are the results of these single studies replicable by another analyst using the same materials. As a practical matter, this hinders the ability to integrate the study of individuals within general theories of social action, and so assess their causal weight relative to actor-general variables.[2] There are also formidable problems, in the absence of even the possibility of replicating the original analysis, in ensuring that the biases and viewpoints of the analyst do not overly influence the portrait constructed of the individual – the problem of the portrait that tells us more about the painter than the subject.

Fortunately, so-called 'remote assessment techniques', employing quantitative content analysis of the words spoken by political leaders, have recently offered the promise of substantially mitigating these difficulties.[3] Remote assessment utilizes 'words as data', regarding public domain texts produced by political leaders not as artefacts to be interrogated to reveal underlying discourses, but as raw data that are amenable to systematic analysis and can tell us something of interest about their authors. The use of political texts in this way carries significant research advantages and, as Laver, Benoit and Garry note, is increasingly popular across the discipline:

> Political texts are the concrete by-product of strategic political activity and have a widely recognized potential to reveal important information about … their authors. Moreover, they can be analyzed, reanalyzed, and reanalyzed again without becoming jaded or uncooperative. Once a text and an analysis technique are placed in the public domain, furthermore, others can replicate, modify, and improve the estimates involved or can produce completely new analyses using the same tools. Above all, in a world where vast volumes of text are easily, cheaply, and almost instantly available, the systematic analysis of political text has the potential to be immensely liberating for the researcher.[4]

If we can make something of the words spoken in public by politicians, then problems of access become much less significant.

Further, remote assessment content analysis techniques can mitigate the problems of conceptualization and measurement that have stymied the study of individuals. The discipline necessary to construct content analytic schemes has gone a long way toward introducing consistency in the study of individual characteristics, and sharpening the underlying conceptualizations. As Winter notes, the progress towards objective measurement and solid evidence has been striking when compared with the more traditional psycho-biographical methods, and consistent conceptualization and measurement provide a solid ground for inference concerning behavioural outcomes.[5] Simply put, with reliable data it is possible to compare the behaviour of individuals with different measured characteristics faced with similar situations, and to build up a body of empirically supported propositions concerning the effect of personality on politics.[6] Access becomes a matter of securing words spoken directly by politicians – a much lower hurdle to surmount than relying on being able to interview them directly. Comparability and cumulation are also eased – comparison can be made rather precisely through quantitative data, and a cumulative body of hypotheses can be generated, and tested, concerning the correlation between data produced by the content analysis and observed behaviours.

Trait analysis

A major application of remote assessment has been 'trait analysis', a scheme focused upon the leader's politically relevant predispositions towards the international environment. The originator of the approach, Margaret G. Hermann, was trained in both psychology and political science and developed from the literature of both fields a set of variables that represented a leader's approach to fundamental problems of politics and political action. Several of these variables focused upon *cognitive content*, representing beliefs held by the individual about how the political world works. Others focused upon *cognitive style*, indicating a stable way of processing and organizing information about the world. A final component was *motivations*, those factors that drive the individual's actions in the political world. I utilize variables from each of these categories in assessing the worldview and leadership style of Tony Blair.

Belief in ability to control events represents the 'locus of control' of the individual. A low score on this variable indicates an external locus of control: the individual believes themselves and their state to be subject to the actions of others and broad historical trends, and perceives that they are relatively unable to alter the course of events. Effort therefore tends to be focused upon managing the consequences of the actions of others in a reactive fashion. These individuals have been found to be disposed towards more cautious and contingent foreign policies. By contrast, a higher score on this variable indicates an 'internal' locus of control: the individual perceives themselves to be efficacious in relation to their political environment, and perceives that their state is an influential political actor. They see themselves as persuasive and are optimistic as to the chances of achieving their goals. Barriers to action are surmountable with a sufficient application of will. These beliefs can lead to the challenging of environmental constraints upon action,[7] expansionist or interventionist foreign policy orientations,[8] and preferences for more active, less deliberative decision processes.[9] Of course, the perception of the degree of control over events may well be inaccurate. A false belief in low control can cause leaders to miss opportunities to shape events to their advantage, while a false belief in high control can lead to over-reach. The issue, then, is not the 'objective' malleability of the external environment, but rather the subjective representation of the environment within the individual's information processing system.

A second trait, *conceptual complexity*, focuses upon the degree of differentiation an individual perceives in the environment in which they operate. This is a structural attribute of an individual's information processing style, rather than a specific belief about an aspect of the world.[10] Lower complexity individuals operate with a more black-and-white information processing system, perceiving international politics and actors as falling into relatively straightforward categories: 'us and them', 'friend or enemy', 'good and evil'. These individuals form strong schematic representations of their environment, are less likely to reconsider the fundamental assumptions of policy, and are slower to perceive evidence that does not fit with their preconceptions. Lower complexity individuals have been found to be comfortable making decisions based upon a restricted information search,[11] and there is some evidence of a link between lower complexity and a more aggressive foreign policy.[12] Tetlock, in an extended examination of the complexity of an individual's worldview and their capacity for good judgment in politics, terms these individuals 'hedgehogs': they know one thing and stick to it relentlessly.[13] By contrast, higher complexity individuals operate with more nuanced information processing systems, perceiving international politics and actors not in Manichean, black-and-white terms but as multiple 'shades of grey'. These individuals require more information prior to making a decision, and are less likely to commit themselves to an irreversible course of action. Tetlock terms these individuals 'foxes': subtly picking their way toward their goals. It is important to note that higher complexity information processing will not necessarily lead to better decisions, let alone outcomes, when compared with lower complexity, and that the variable is empirical rather than normative. Indeed, under many circumstances, lower complexity can be adaptive – such as when one faces an implacable foe whose intentions are unclear.

The third trait considered is *need for power*. This draws upon the psychology of motivation in human action. Individuals are driven by certain needs, including achievement, affiliation with similar individuals or groups, and, as here, the need to exert domination or control.[14] As an adaptation of this basic insight to politics, the need for power variable indicates that individuals with higher scores tend to require greater personal control and involvement in policy, and are more likely to insist that policy outputs match their personal preferences rather than represent consensual group decisions. Preston found this tendency to be acute in studies of US presidents and their advisory groups, noting that presidents who scored highly restricted their advisory groups to small gatherings of like-minded officials, while circumventing more regularized decision-making structures. By contrast, leaders lower in the need for power are more comfortable with delegating decision power and control of the agenda, and seek to reach consensus among those with responsibility for policy rather than impose their own will regardless of the views of others.[15] Hermann adds that need for power is often associated not just with the desire to control others, but also the skill of an individual in doing so – individuals scoring higher often show highly developed tactical skills in manipulating events to their advantage.[16]

Method

The measurement of these personality traits relies upon a content analysis of the words spoken by the individual in question, on the assumption that 'thought processes underlie spoken or written communication', and that it is reasonable to infer that 'the (thought) process and the (spoken or written) product are related and that the product reflects some important aspects of the process'.[17] Coding dictionaries associated with the traits are used to scan text for words or phrases associated with a positive or negative manifestation of the trait in question. A 'score' for an individual is the ratio of positive to negative 'hits' within the spoken material. The fundamental assumption, therefore, is that 'the more frequently leaders use certain words and phrases ... the more salient such content is to them'.[18] Coding for *belief in ability to control events* focuses upon verbs that reflect action or the planning of action by the leader and their state. Coding for *conceptual complexity* focuses upon words that indicate nuance and differentiation (i.e. 'approximately', 'possibility', 'trend'), versus words indicative of absolutist or dichotomous thinking ('certainly', 'definitely', 'irreversibly'). Finally, coding for *need for power* focuses upon the assertion of dominance of the individual or the individual's state over others in the political environment. To give an example, the sentence

'I will certainly invade Iraq'

contains three data points. 'I will', as an indicator of action, would be recorded as a positive measurement of *belief in ability to control events*. 'Certainly', as an indicator of less nuanced information processing, would be recorded as a negative measure of *conceptual complexity*. 'Invade', as an indicator of assertive actions over another, would be recorded as a positive measure of *need for power*. As the volume of text coded increases, thousands of data points accumulate and a picture of an individual as relatively higher or lower on these traits emerges.

While early iterations of the technique focused upon the hand-coding of material, advances in both desktop computing and the availability of electronic text have lent themselves to the automation of the process. A dedicated software program for conducting the content analysis, 'Profiler Plus', is now commonly used. This eliminates inter-rater reliability concerns, as the computer perfectly reproduces the analysis of a given set of materials each time.

The material analysed in this study was the universe of Blair's responses to parliamentary questions from 5 May 1997 (his first day in office) until 27 June 2007 (his last), available through the *Hansard's Parliamentary Debates* series: a verbatim record of every word spoken in the British House of Commons. The frequency of questioning of the prime minister and the decade-long time span means that the profile of Blair is based upon over 230,000 words, containing many thousands of coding opportunities. In order to provide a reference group against which to compare Blair's scores, these procedures were repeated for each British prime minister from 1945 on.[19]

The use of responses to parliamentary questions as source material carries important advantages that can increase our confidence in the results. First, responses to questions are relatively spontaneous, reducing the risks, inherent in the use of set-piece speeches, that heavy editing and drafting by speechwriters has occurred. While the prime minister can make an educated guess about the topics upon which they will receive questions, and can begin to organize their thoughts before-hand, they have no way of knowing the precise thrust of the question nor from whom it will come. Further, use of parliamentary questions provides a means to control for some potentially troubling sources of variation that would be implicated in the use of other materials, such as television interviews or speeches to various domestic and interna-tional groups. These materials can be subject to audience and to format effects that may distort the results obtained.

In order to track the degree of stability in Blair's scores over time – and to check against the concern that the trait scores may be highly random without obvious pattern – the parliamentary responses were organized into annual groupings. This unit of analysis provides a good number of observations while preserving a sufficient volume of mate-rial to form the basis for each measurement.

Results

Table 3.1 reports the results. On the *belief in ability to control events* variable, Blair's mean score of .44 is significantly higher than the refer-ence group mean of .31, indicating that Blair is a positive outlier on

Table 3.1 *Tony Blair's trait scores and a reference group of post-1945 British prime ministers*

	British prime ministers 1945–97	Tony Blair 1997–2007	1997	1998	1999	2000	2001	2002	2003	2004	2005	2006	2007
Belief in ability to control events	.31	.44	.42	.45	.46	.49	.42	.43	.45	.40	.42	.44	.43
Conceptual complexity	.55	.51	.51	.49	.48	.56	.50	.52	.49	.52	.52	.52	.54
Need for power	.22	.28	.29	.28	.29	.40	.29	.27	.28	.23	.24	.28	.33
Number of words coded	732,722	230,333	8,123	17,922	23,075	6,792	24,502	32,280	31,364	44,565	10,400	19,595	11,715

this variable in comparison with others who have held the post. A high score on *belief in ability to control events* leads us to predict from Blair a proactive policy stance with a relatively low weighting of the environmental constraints upon political action in his decision calculus, and a perception of personal efficacy in international affairs.

On the *conceptual complexity* measure, Blair is again an outlier, this time in a negative direction, his mean score being .51 compared with the .55 mean of post-1945 prime ministers. Being substantially lower than the mean for modern prime ministers on conceptual complexity, we would expect from Blair a straightforward information processing style, characterized by limited search and an emphasis on binary classifications, a decisive orientation with a minimum of debate and discussion, and a relatively low frequency of re-examination of the assumptions of policies.

Finally, Blair's mean score of .28 on the *need for power* variable is significantly higher than the reference group mean of .22. With his higher need for power, we would expect Blair to be heavily involved in all aspects of policy formation, and to shape an advisory and decision process based upon small groups of hand-picked individuals, relegating formal structures such as the cabinet and the Foreign Office to essentially 'rubber-stamp' roles.

The Blair style

As a check on the validity of this portrait of Blair, and as a way to flesh out and contextualize the picture of his worldview and leadership style, we can examine the views of the prime minister's colleagues and biographers. Does the picture of Blair generated by remote assessment techniques fit with the judgments of those who know or have studied the prime minister?

Considering first Blair's high measured belief in ability to control events, colleagues and observers agree that Blair is an extremely proactive prime minister, with a propensity to discount the barriers to taking action and effecting change. 'He's got that sense of mission in his underlying psychology', says Sir Jeremy Greenstock.[20] The core of his foreign policy, according to close ally David Blunkett, is that 'he's interventionist'.[21] Chris Smith, a former cabinet minister, agrees that Blair's philosophy can be 'characterized as a duty to intervene, even when the direct interests of the UK are not being threatened'.[22] Kampfner argues that he 'acquired a passion for military intervention without precedent in modern British political history and without parallel internationally'.[23] Blair realizes, says Lord Guthrie, the head of the British armed forces from 1997–2001, 'that the world is a dangerous place, that if you do absolutely nothing, it is likely to get more dangerous'. He is not perturbed, Guthrie notes, by 'doing things that may in the short term be very dangerous and difficult politically'.[24]

His seminal enunciation of a foreign affairs philosophy was, as we shall see in Chapter 4, profoundly forward-leaning. The central problem in international affairs, he suggested, is 'when to get involved in other people's conflicts'.[25] Blair's view is that the strong and the democratic – especially the Untied States acting with the full support of its British ally – have a duty to remake the world in their image for the benefit of all people: 'those that can act, must', said Blair to the 2001 Labour Party Conference.[26]

This sense of mission is underlined by a great degree of self-confidence and belief in his personal efficacy. 'Tony is the great persuader', a close aide comments. 'He thinks he can convert people even when it might seem as if he doesn't have a cat in hell's chance of succeeding. Call him naïve, call it what you will, but he never gives up. He would say things like "I can get Jacques (Chirac) to do this" or "leave Putin to me".' A French official, noting the same tendency, suggests that 'there is not a single problem that Blair thinks he cannot solve with his own personal engagement – it could be Russia, it could be Africa'. This high belief in personal efficacy does come with the risk of over-reach, however: 'the trouble is, the world is a little more complicated than that.'[27] For Blair, though, success is a matter of personal investment in a problem. As Matthew D'Ancona puts it, 'Blair is a natural participator. He sees a line and he runs towards it. He sees a club and he wants to join it. He sees a campaign and he wants to be a part of it.'[28] He has, Seldon says, an 'almost limitless belief in his ability to persuade', but these are powers he has tended to 'exaggerate greatly'.[29]

The low conceptual complexity score again fits well with other observations of the prime minister. Blair is seen to have a clarity of worldview, a tendency to see issues in black and white rather than shades of grey, that is so vivid as to have been termed 'Manichean'. 'You have to remember', a Downing Street insider comments, 'that the PM is a conviction politician.' His biographer Anthony Seldon agrees: 'his very certainty often militated against him seeing other truths and perspectives.'[30] Seldon continues: 'He conceptualizes the world as a struggle between good and evil in which his particular vocation is to advance the former.'[31] Lord Guthrie judges that Blair 'believed in making the world a better place. He thinks if good men do nothing, bad men prevail. He is driven by that.'[32]

This tendency toward the drawing of stark alternatives has led, in the judgment of colleagues and observers, to a comfort with division of the world into 'them and us' categories with strong moralistic underpinnings. 'No European leader of his generation', Danchev notes 'speaks so unblushingly of good and evil'.[33] Blair has an 'instinctive moralism'.[34] His worldview, according to close ally David Blunkett, is about 'doing the right thing and doing good, and not tolerating evil'.[35] His one time political mentor, the former Labour home secretary Roy Jenkins, said of him 'My view is that the prime minister, far from lacking conviction, has almost too much, particularly when dealing with the world beyond Britain. He is a little too Manichean for my perhaps now jaded taste, seeing matters in stark terms of good and evil, black and white.'[36] He has, judges Sir Jeremy Greenstock, 'a very strong sense of sticking to his guns when he thinks he's got the right approach.'[37]

There have been suggestions that this is a worldview rooted in Blair's religious faith – which is unusually strong for a British prime minister. D'Ancona suggests that 'Blair's entire political behaviour has to be linked to his private religious beliefs … it's impossible to see one without the other'.[38] Paul Hoggart concurs, arguing that Blair's foreign policy is based on 'powerful illusions touching on imminence, teleology, and salvation' through which the prime minister's 'religiosity found expression in the secular field of global politics'.[39] However, religiosity in itself seems a poor explanation for foreign policy. Many people of faith have bitterly opposed elements of Blair's agenda, most famously the Iraq war. What seems more reasonable is to say that Blair's particular interpretation of morality is based on stark judgments of good and evil, and is consistent with an overall worldview that tends toward the absolutist. As Blair himself wrote in the foreword to a collection of essays on faith and politics:

> Christianity is a very tough religion: it is judgmental. There is right and wrong. There is good and bad. We all know this, of course, but it has become fashionable to be uncomfortable about such language. But when we look at our world today and how much needs to be done, we should not hesitate to make such judgments.[40]

The salient point, as William Shawcross notes, is not that Blair's faith drives his foreign policy, but that his interpretation of issues of morality and faith is very clear: '[t]here is, of course, far more to Blair's decision making than his religion. But he brought his views of right and wrong to the conduct of Britain's foreign policy.'[41] As Blair himself put it, 'I am a practicing Christian and that's part of me – there's no point in denying it'. While not 'trying to wear God on [my] sleeve or paint God into the picture', Blair had resolved that 'religious belief wasn't something that shut you away from the world, but something that meant you had to go out and act'.[42]

Perhaps as a consequence of this tendency to see the world in clear-cut, broad-brush terms, Blair is disinterested in policy detail, and does not like to engage in minutiae or to struggle with the complexities of an issue.[43] As Clare Short notes, 'he's read very little history, or very little on recent politics. He's not stupid, but he doesn't do detail on policy either.'[44] For James Naughtie, a biographer and observer, it is clear that he 'prefers the sweep of a broad canvas to the politics of detail'.[45] Derek Scott, a former adviser, notes that Blair 'focuses on the big picture, and in pursuit of his longer-term goals he may be less fastidious than some with narrower preoccupations'.[46]

The high score on *need for power* also finds recognition among observers and colleagues of Blair. An aspect of his style often commented upon is the preference for personalistic government and tightly held policy processes, with a consequent disdain for cabinet, cabinet committees, and formal meetings.[47] This style was immortalized in the key 'Butler report' on Iraq decision making as 'sofa government', an ad hoc set of processes based around the prime minister and aides making decisions outside of the formal machinery of government. Anthony Seldon pithily characterized Blair's governing style as 'denocracy', based upon seclusion of himself and a few close aides in a Downing Street private study known as 'the den'. Decisions could be made quickly in the den, and time-consuming processes of consultation – and potentially the airing of dissenting voices – could be minimized. Derek Scott, an adviser to Blair, reports that '[m]eetings were generally informal rather than businesslike with the principal participants scattered on one of the couches'.[48] Cabinet, of course, continued to meet, but became increasingly sidelined in terms of genuine discussion and decision making. Peter Hennessy, who has studied cabinet operation in the modern premiership, records that 'the Blair cabinets were extraordinary affairs and not just because of their brevity. There was no proper agenda',[49] while a senior Whitehall figure suggests that 'the PM doesn't like argument. Cabinet these days is just a series of self-congratulatory remarks.'[50] Riddell writes that he 'regarded weekly meetings of the cabinet as a brief reporting session, seldom long enough for a cup of coffee'.[51]

This reflected both impatience with formal and institutionalized decision making and a desire to exercise personal control over policy. Upon taking office, close aides of Blair warned members of the government that they would not be allowed to operate like 'feudal barons', but instead would be subject to 'Napoleonic' central control,[52] while another Blair aide characterized the preferred mode of government as a 'unitary command structure'.[53] Blair's 'inner circle was small and there was not much more than a nod to the notion of collective decision making'.[54] Clare Short states bluntly that in Blair's government, 'collegial style there was not', a mode of operation that, in her judgment, 'explains some of the deficiencies of decision making'.[55] Blunkett agrees that Blair prefers streamlined decision processes, but suggests this was an adaptive rather than deficient means of conducting government:

> Tony didn't like the worst elements of the formal structure which actually take an enormous amount of time but don't end up going anywhere … Margaret Thatcher and Tony Blair were alike in being impatient in going through convoluted, detailed procedural mechanisms which had very little to do with good decision making and everything to do with actually going through a performance and a theatre.[56]

Blair's preference for personal control is also part of the reason for his interest in foreign affairs: domestic politics is negotiation, bureaucracy, incrementalism, whereas foreign affairs more readily lends itself to giving a strong lead and direct decision making. Tied to this, observers judge, was the constraint upon Blair's domestic freedom of action caused by the troubled relationship with the chancellor, Gordon Brown. Blair and Brown had reached an accommodation, closely connected to Brown agreeing not to challenge Blair for leadership of the Labour party in the mid-1990s, that as chancellor, Brown would exercise broad control over much of the detail of domestic politics.[57] In return, he would play no role in foreign policy.[58] This is not a mere practical deal however – Blair genuinely prefers the world stage to domestic politics because the issues tend to suit his style: 'the choice between good and evil is often much clearer abroad than in his struggles at home.'[59]

The evidence from Blair's colleagues and biographers therefore lends strong support to the profile of the prime minister developed through the trait analysis. We now have multiple sources of evidence converging around a picture of the prime minister as highly proactive and confident, with a clear-cut, black and white worldview, and a preference for tightly held, non-consultative decision processes.

Tony Blair's leadership style in comparative perspective

One of the benefits of remote assessment trailed at the beginning of the chapter was the possibility for systematic comparison across political leaders. Indeed, we can set the scores for Blair within a wider context by considering the behaviours theoretically associated with this configuration of personality traits, and the record of previous research into individuals with these characteristics. While these vignettes of leaders and foreign policy episodes are obviously more illustrative than definitive, they do serve to bolster the argument that is being made about the Blair style and its impact on policy.

Belief in ability to control events and adventuristic leadership: Eden and suez

Blair is substantially higher in *belief in ability to control events* than both the average British prime minister and the average world leader. In terms of post-1945 British prime ministers, Anthony Eden scores most similarly to Blair.[60] Eden, of course, famously followed a highly interventionist foreign policy course in the Suez crisis, an episode that is sometimes compared with Blair's Iraq decision making. Indeed, the comparison is illuminating in terms of illustrating the hypothesized behaviours associated with leaders who score highly on this trait.

The 1956 crisis revolved around the seizure of the Suez Canal by Egyptian leader Gamal Abdul Nasser. On hearing of the seizure, Eden's immediate response was innately proactive, as he sought to launch a rapid military operation to recapture the canal, and was hugely disappointed that no such option was logistically possible.[61] Eden fretted his way through diplomatic niceties, but was desperate to do something positive to settle the crisis. He therefore listened attentively when the French explained a plan they had concocted for an Israeli attack on Egypt, which would appear to threaten the security of the canal. The French and the British would issue an ultimatum to both sides to halt the fighting – with Israeli compliance secured by prior collusion. French and British troops could then enter the canal zone as 'peacekeepers' to protect its operation, with the happy side effect of leaving their forces in control of the canal. The combined impact of an Israeli invasion and the entry of French and British troops would so humiliate Nasser as to cause his government to fall. This was a plan of the highest ambition and proactivity, relying on an implausibly long list of events and reactions breaking Eden's way: a successful Israeli invasion, the ability to keep collusion between Israel, Britain and France secret, the acquiescence of the United States and the United Nations, and the ability of UK-French forces to rapidly capture and hold a substantial slice of Egyptian territory. That Eden believed he could shape so many separate factors illustrates the tendency toward over-reach characteristic of leaders who score highly on the belief in ability to control events variable.

Once set in motion many in the United Nations and, crucially, the United States, saw through the ruse. Eisenhower, alarmed by Eden's adventurism, began to withhold the financial aid upon which the unstable British currency depended, and Eden had no choice but to halt operations.

The significance of the episode in the current context is the hugely ambitious and proactive policy solution Eden, with his high belief in ability to control events, had settled upon. While of course not every leader who scores highly on this trait will experience their own 'Suez', the degree to which Eden perceived himself as able to shape events in ways that others thought unlikely is a characteristic of this type of leader. As we will later see, this is a characteristic Blair exhibited throughout his ten years in office.

Conceptual complexity and black-and-white thinking:
Thatcher and the Falklands

Blair is substantially lower than the average prime minister and the average world leader in his conceptual complexity score. Compared with other British prime ministers, Blair is most similar to Margaret Thatcher, a famously black-and-white thinker.[62] With Thatcher, Anthony King noted a 'disposition to see the political world as divided into friends and enemies, goodies and baddies',[63] while Francis Pym, the former foreign secretary, found that 'she likes everything to be clear-cut: absolutely in favour of one thing, absolutely against another'.[64]

These decision-making tendencies were strongly in evidence during the Falklands crisis, the major foreign policy event of her tenure. The Argentinean invasion of 2 April 1982 came as a surprise to the British government, but Thatcher responded in characteristically clear fashion: 'we have got to get them back.'[65] She very quickly framed the situation in black-and-white terms of Argentinean aggression and British virtue. Accompanying this was a resistance to a compromise diplomatic solution, and a belief that ultimately military force would be necessary. Thatcher rejected the counsel of the Foreign Office, and especially her diplomatically minded foreign secretary, Francis Pym:

> I received advice from the Foreign Office which summed up the flexibility of principle characteristic of that department. I was presented with the dangers of a backlash against the British expatriates in Argentina, problems about getting support in the UN Security Council, the lack of reliance we could place on the European Community or the United States, the risk of the Soviets becoming involved, the disadvantage of being looked at as a colonial power. All these considerations were fair enough. But when you are at war you cannot allow the difficulties to dominate your thinking. You have to set out with an iron will to overcome them. And anyway what was the alternative? That a common or garden dictator should rule over the Queen's subjects and prevail by fraud and violence? Not while I was Prime Minister.[66]

The American secretary of state Alexander Haig, dispatched by President Reagan to try to avoid a shooting war between the major US ally in Europe and the major US ally in Latin America, received similar treatment from Thatcher's Manichean mindset. Haig, received in the drawing room at 10 Downing Street, found Thatcher in determined mode and in the grip of dubious historical analogies:

> after I had explained the American proposals to Mrs Thatcher, she rapped sharply on the tabletop and recalled that this was the table at which Neville Chamberlain sat in 1938 and spoke of the Czechs as a faraway people about whom we know so little and with whom we have so little in common. A world war and the death of over 45 million people followed. She begged us to remember this: Do not urge Britain to reward aggression, to give Argentina something taken by force that it could not attain by peaceful means ... She was in a forceful mood, embattled, incisive.[67]

Thatcher remained concerned throughout the crisis with an essentially monochrome framing of events focused around the need to subordinate diplomacy to an essentially military timetable. Negotiations would not resolve the conflict, and their sole purpose was to buy time for the British naval taskforce to position itself around the islands. Diplomatic proposals, right up to the beginning of fighting, were rejected by Thatcher, who felt they were simply attempts to obfuscate by the

Argentine government, accepted at face value by a naïve and spineless British foreign office. The Falklands crisis was therefore resolved by force, culminating in the Argentine surrender in the Islands' capital city of Port Stanley on 12 June.

Thatcher's decision-making style and behaviour in the Falklands crisis is a vivid example of some of the characteristics of individuals scoring lower on conceptual complexity: division of the world into stark categories of 'them and us', 'good and evil', and a propensity to discount alternatives to the course of action originally settled upon or to reconsider the fundamental principals and assumptions of a policy. While Thatcher and Blair were in many ways very different politicians, their foreign policy behaviours did often share this basic tendency.

Need for power and tight control of decision making: Lyndon Johnson and Vietnam

Thomas Preston examined the need for power trait across several American presidents, and his work can provide some useful comparative perspective on Blair's high score.[68] In particular, Preston found that Harry Truman, Dwight Eisenhower, John F. Kennedy and Lyndon Johnson scored highly on this trait, and all preferred advisory systems based around small group processes, allowing the president to maintain a tight control over decision making. Lyndon Johnson, in particular, exhibited this style during the prolonged US intervention in Vietnam. Preston quotes former secretary of state Dean Rusk as stating that 'As far as Vietnam is concerned, President Johnson was his own desk officer' while former secretary of defense Robert McNamara found his style 'autocratic'. Johnson would centralize decision making into his tightly held 'Tuesday lunch' group, composed of aides and associates who tended to reinforce his existing predispositions on Vietnam.[69] More regularized decision-making bodies such as the National Security Council and the full cabinet became essentially rubber-stamps on decisions made elsewhere.[70] This tendency led to pathologies in information processing – Johnson was a voracious reader and aggressively probed those around him for information, but his decision processes were so narrowly focused, and his experience in international affairs so limited, that he tended to be fed information from a narrow band of like-minded individuals.[71] It is perhaps unsurprising, therefore, that it took several years of deterioration in the Vietnam situation before Johnson began to reconsider the fundamental tenets of the policy.

The above is not to suggest that Blair is some chimerical composite of Margaret Thatcher, Lyndon Johnson, and Anthony Eden. Obviously, Blair and the situations he faced differed in many ways from the three portraits presented above. Nonetheless, the value of the systematic procedures for measuring personality lies in the ability to make reliable measurement of individual characteristics, and to compare individuals who may at first glance appear very different in terms of ideology, country of origin, and policy goals. While Blair is similar to other political leaders when the traits individually are addressed, he is unique in the combination of a very high belief in ability to control events, low conceptual complexity, and high need for power. It is this combination of traits that underpins the 'Blair style' as a worldview and approach to international affairs.

Conclusion

Having developed the case in the previous chapter that the style and worldviews of individuals are significant causal variables and can be systematically incorporated into theories of international politics, we have built upon that argument in several ways in this chapter. The commonly stated objections to the study of the individual – that it is formidably difficult and unlikely to result in scientific progress in any real sense of the term – have been shown to be serious but not insurmountable. A technique for harnessing the loquacity of politicians to research ends has been introduced and applied to Blair, and a portrait of his leadership style – proactive, based upon stark categorizations, personalistic and directive – has been elaborated. This portrait corresponds quite nicely with the recollections and observations of those who have studied Blair with more everyday methods, and I have elaborated on the ways in which Blair's style is different from and similar to other British prime ministers and world leaders.

The preliminaries complete, we can in the subsequent chapters apply our hypotheses concerning how a leader with Blair's characteristics would act in a unipolar system, leading a state allied to the hegemon, and faced with threats from rogue states and terrorist groups. We begin with Blair's first major foray into international affairs: the Kosovo crisis.

Notes

1 A. George and J. George, *Woodrow Wilson and Colonel House* (New York: Dover, 1964).

2 C. Taber, 'Problems of empirical inference in elite decision making', *The Political Psychologist*, 5:1 (2000), 511–27.

3 M. Schafer, 'Issues in assessing psychological characteristics at-a-distance: Symposium lessons and future research directions', *Political Psychology*, 21:3 (2000), 512.

4 M. Laver, K. Benoit and J. Garry, 'Extracting policy positions from political text using words as data', *American Political Science Review*, 97:2 (2003), 311–31.

5 D. G. Winter, 'Assessing leader's personalities: a historical survey of academic research studies', in J. M. Post (ed.), *The Psychological Assessment of Political Leaders* (Ann Arbor, MI: University of Michigan Press, 2003), p. 21.

6 J. Post, S. G. Walker and D. G. Winter, 'Profiling political leaders: an introduction', in J. M. Post (ed.), *The Psychological Assessment of Political Leaders* (Ann Arbor, MI: University of Michigan Press, 2003), p. 4.

7 M. G. Hermann, 'Assessing leadership style: trait analysis', in J. M. Post (ed.), *The Psychological Assessment of Political Leaders* (Ann Arbor, MI: University of Michigan Press, 2003), pp. 178–214.

8 J. Kaarbo and M. G. Hermann, 'Leadership styles of prime ministers: how individual differences affect the foreign policy process', *Leadership Quarterly*, 9:3 (1998), 252–3.

9 T. Preston, 'Following the leader: the impact of US presidential style upon advisery group dynamics, structure, and decision', in P. t'Hart, B. Sundelius, E. Stern (eds), *Beyond Groupthink: Group Decision-Making in Foreign Policy* (Ann Arbor. MI: University of Michigan Press, 1997), pp. 191–248.

10 Y. Y. I. Vertzberger, *The World in Their Minds: Information Processing, Cognition, and Perception in Foreign Policy Decisionmaking* (Stanford, CA: Stanford University Press, 1990), p. 133.

11 T. Preston, *The President and his Inner Circle: Leadership Style and the Advisory Process in Foreign Affairs* (New York: Columbia University Press, 2001); P. Kowert, *Groupthink or Deadlock: When do Leaders Learn from Their Advisers?* (Albany, NY: SUNY Press, 2002).

12 M. G. Hermann, 'Explaining foreign policy behavior using the personal characteristics of political leaders', *International Studies Quarterly*, 24:1 (1980), 40; P. Suedfeld and P. E. Tetlock, 'Integrative complexity of communication in international crisis', *Journal of Conflict Resolution*, 21 (1977) 169–84.

13 P. E. Tetlock, *Expert Political Judgement: How Good is It? How Can we Know?* (Princeton, NJ: Princeton University Press, 2005).

14 D. G. Winter, 'Leader appeal, leader performance, and the motive profiles of leaders and followers: a study of American presidents and elections', *Journal of Personality and Social Psychology*, 52:1 (1987), 196–202; D. G. Winter, 'Personality and foreign policy', in E. Singer and V. Hobson

(eds), *Political Psychology and Foreign Policy* (Boulder, CO: Westview, 1987), pp. 79–101; D. G. Winter, 'Power, affiliation, and war: three tests of a motivational model', *Journal of Personality and Social Psychology*, 65:3 (1993), 532–45.

15 Preston, *The President and his Inner Circle.*

16 Hermann, 'Assessing leadership style', pp. 195–6.

17 P. Suedfeld, K. Guttieri and P. E. Tetlock, 'Assessing integrative complexity at a distance: archival analyses of thinking and decision making', in J. M. Post (ed.), *The Psychological Assessment of Political Leaders* (Ann Arbor, MI: University of Michigan Press, 2003) pp. 246–70.

18 Hermann, 'Assessing leadership style', p. 186

19 These data are reported fully for the 'conceptual complexity' variable in S. B. Dyson, 'Text annotation and the cognitive architecture of political leaders: British prime ministers from 1945–2008', *Journal of Information Technology and Politics* (forthcoming).

20 Author interview with Sir Jeremy Greenstock, 6 June 2007.

21 Author interview with David Blunkett, 1 May 2007.

22 Author interview with Chris Smith, 18 June 2007.

23 J. Kampfner, *Blair's Wars* (London: Simon & Schuster, 2004).

24 Author interview with Lord Guthrie, 20 June 2007.

25 Tony Blair, 'The Doctrine of the International Community', speech to the Economic Club, Chicago, 24 April 1999. Available at www.pm.gov.uk/output/Page1297.asp, accessed 3 July 2007.

26 Blair speech to the 2001 Labour Party Conference. Available at www.ppionline.org/ppi_ci.cfm?knlgAreaID=128&subsecID=187&contentID=3881, accessed 14 July 2007.

27 Kampfner, *Blair's Wars*, pp. 127–8.

28 *Frontline*, interview with Matthew D'Ancona, 11 March 2003. Available www.pbs.org/wgbh/pages/frontline/shows/blair/interviews/dancona. html, accessed 3 July 2007.

29 A. Seldon, *Blair* (London: Free Press, 2004), p. 698–9.

30 Ibid., p. 599.

31 Ibid., p. 700.

32 Author interview with Lord Guthrie, 20 June 2007.

33 A. Danchev, 'I'm with you: Tony Blair and the obligations of alliance: Anglo-American relations in historical perspective', in L. C. Gardner and M. B. Young (eds), *Iraq and the Lessons of Vietnam* (New York: The New Press, 2007), p. 48

34 P. Riddell, *The Unfulfilled Prime Minister: Tony Blair's Quest for a Legacy* (London: Politico's, 2006), p. 14.

35 Author interview with David Blunkett, 1 May 2007.

36 J. Naughtie, *The Accidental American: Tony Blair and the Presidency* (New York: Public Affairs, 2004), p. 135.

37 Author interview with Sir Jeremy Greenstock, 6 June 2007.

38 *Frontline*, interview with Matthew D'Ancona.

39 P. Hoggett, 'Iraq: Blair's mission impossible', *British Journal of Politics and International Relations*, 7:4 (2005), 418.

40 Quoted in Kampfner, *Blair's Wars*, p. 74.

41 W. Shawcross, *Allies: The US, Britain, Europe and the War in Iraq* (New York: Public Affairs, 2003), p. 47.

42 Quoted in M. Cockerell, 'An inside view on Blair's number 10', in A. Seldon (ed.), *The Blair Effect* (London: Little, Brown 2001), p. 573.

43 Peter Riddell, 'Blair as prime minister' in Seldon (ed.), *The Blair Effect*, p. 35.

44 Author interview with Clare Short, 30 April 2007.

45 Naughtie, *The Accidental American*, p. xv.

46 D. Scott, *Off Whitehall: A View from Downing Street by Tony Blair's Adviser* (New York: I. B. Tauris, 2004), p. 20.

47 Riddell, 'Blair as prime minister', p. 32.

48 Scott, *Off Whitehall*, p. 15.

49 P. Hennessy, *The Prime Minister: The Office and its Holders Since 1945* (New York: Penguin, 2000), p. 481.

50 Hennessy, *The Prime Minister*, p. 545

51 Riddell, *The Unfulfilled Prime Minister*, p. 43

52 Hennessy, *The Prime Minister*, p. 478

53 J. Rentoul, *Tony Blair, Prime Minister* (London: Warner Books, 2001), p. 544.

54 Naughtie, *The Accidental American*, p. 47

55 Author interview with Clare Short, 30 April 2007.

56 Author interview with David Blunkett, 1 May 2007.

57 Scott, *Off Whitehall*, pp. 9, 31

58 Seldon, *Blair*, p. 680

59 Seldon, *Blair*, p. 701

60 Eden's mean belief in ability to control events score across his time in office was .38, compared with the mean for all prime ministers of .31.

61 K. Kyle, *Suez* (New York: St Martin's Press, 1991). pp. 135–7.

62 Thatcher's mean complexity score across her time in office was .49, compared with the mean for all prime ministers of .55. For a full account of the impact of Thatcher's cognitive style on Britain's external relations, see S. B. Dyson, 'Cognitive style and foreign policy: Margaret Thatcher's black-and-white thinking', forthcoming in *International Political Science Review*.

63 A. King, 'Margaret Thatcher: the style of a prime minister', in A. King, (ed.), *The British Prime Minister* (London: Macmillan, 1985), p. 132.

64 F. Pym, *The Politics of Consent* (London: Hamish Hamilton, 1984).

65 M. Thatcher, *The Downing Street Years* (New York: HarperCollins, 1993), p. 179.

66 Thatcher, *The Downing Street Years*, p. 181.

67 A. Haig, *Caveat: Realism, Reagan, and Foreign Policy* (New York: Macmillan, 1984), pp. 272–3.

68 Preston, *The President and his Inner Circle*.

69 Ibid., p. 139.

70 Ibid., p. 141.

71 Ibid., p. 148.

4 The Kosovo and Sierra Leone interventions

'There is only one person arguing for ground troops' to go into Kosovo, commented a senior NATO official as the alliance pondered its options, 'and that is Tony Blair'.[1] Blair was indeed alone during late April and May 1999 in pushing forcefully for an invasion of Kosovo to halt Serbian ethnic cleansing operations, and his stance, which was judged by some to be close to 'messianic',[2] provoked high anger from President Clinton, 'widespread bafflement' from the French,[3] and a questioning of his judgment from some cabinet colleagues.

Blair's certainty, proactive stance, and tight control of decision making would be the defining features of his foreign policy, and Kosovo represents their initial manifestation. Further, the war prompted him to elucidate a doctrine of foreign affairs, rooted in his personal worldview, that is key to understanding his later response to the war on terror and the attack on Iraq. Kosovo, in the judgment of John Kampfner, 'transformed the world's view of [Blair] and transformed his view of the world',[4] while to Seldon it represented the final step toward him becoming entrenched in the certainties of his own judgment in foreign affairs.[5] Andrew Rawnsley says it was 'this crucible which began the transformation of the pop star premier into the conviction-driven crusader who would take Britain into war with Iraq'.[6] Rentoul concurs that

> [H]e became more messianic about his foreign policy as a result of his surprising and surprisingly complete vindication in Kosovo. He was told before Kosovo that you can't win wars from the air, there's no point in fighting wars for altruistic motives just to help out relatively small groups of oppressed people. And he was told that it was illegal to interfere in the sovereign affairs of a nation state purely on humanitarian grounds. All those he confounded and he succeeded.[7]

The cabinet minister Clare Short, who would later break with Blair over Iraq, judged that 'he got the taste for military action then'.[8] Kosovo, David Blunkett argues, 'gave him confidence and belief that there was a role to be played by intervention, both in terms of reducing world threat and world tension and the protection of populations literally under dictatorship'.[9] For James Naughtie, 'Historians will argue about the truth of it, but Blair's conviction that his intervention tipped the scales was an important part of his development. He had won a war.'[10]

The Kosovo war

The war in Kosovo, one of a sequence of ethnic conflicts deriving from the break-up of the Yugoslav state, began to attract sustained international attention during late 1998. There was an escalation of the previously low-level conflict between Serb security forces, seeking to enforce the revocation of Kosovo's constitutional autonomy and ultimately to alter the ethnic balance in the territory from its 90% Albanian demographic, and the Kosovo Liberation Army (KLA), a paramilitary organization that had grown frustrated with the passive resistance adopted by the de facto Kosovar leader Ibrahim Rugova. A series of KLA offensives, made possible by the looting of weapons from the chaotic Albanian state contiguous to Kosovo, succeeded in placing swaths of territory beyond the control of Serbian President Slobodan Milosevic's forces. Milosevic responded with counter-offensives which included retributions against Kosovar Albanian civilians. The cycle of violence reached a vivid high in the 15 January massacre at Racak, where Serb forces killed forty-five civilians, with the aftermath beamed into European and American homes and prompting NATO allies into action.

The NATO governments faced a series of dilemmas in approaching the issue, however. While they could not allow Serbian forces to rampage through Kosovo massacring innocents, they also were wary of the KLA, a violent, arguably terroristic, organization. Further, while images of Serb atrocities provoked a public demand for action, NATO governments judged that there was no consensus on what form that action should take, and very little appetite for the insertion of ground forces physically to separate the Kosovo combatants. Consequently, the initial effort was diplomatic in nature, and attempted to replicate the earlier 'Dayton Accords' that had brought the Bosnia-Serbia conflict to a close. This was a phenomenally difficult task, given that Serbian President Milosevic, who was making great domestic capital out of the assertion of Serb nationalism in the historically significant Kosovo territory, showed very little interest in reaching a diplomatic compromise. Further, the Kosovar Albanian side had a split leadership, with the pacifist Rugova, selected twice by the majority population as their leader in elections Milosevic refused to ratify, being rivalled by Hashim Thaci, the militant head of the KLA who saw the violent expulsion of the Serbian presence as the only viable solution.

Two weeks after the Racak massacre, NATO and the 'contact group'[11] announced that both sides must meet to negotiate an acceptable solution based upon Kosovar autonomy, and that talks would be held in the French town of Rambouillet beginning on 6 February and ending one week later. NATO also issued a reluctant-seeming pledge to use force against Serbia should the Rambouillet talks fail.

Rambouillet proved to be a taxing diplomatic assignment for the NATO foreign ministers. Milosevic took the talks unseriously, refusing to attend in person, and sending a second-tier delegation which availed itself of the hospitality on offer and consumed impressive quantities of wine, but invested somewhat less effort in the actual negotiations. The Kosovar delegation was split between Rugova and the implacable Thaci, who sought a maximalist position of immediate independence from Serbia, and refused to agree to any disarmament of the KLA. Madeline Albright, the US secretary of state, quickly realized that agreement with the Serbs was a non-starter, and so concentrated her efforts on gaining the assent of the Kosovars to a set of principles which could then be used to put pressure on Milosevic.[12] Absent the agreement of the Kosovars, it would be difficult for NATO governments to paint Milosevic as a hold-out and to apply coercive pressure upon him. After much effort and employment of diplomatic craft, the Kosovar delegation signed the peace plan on 18 March.

This rather radically narrowed Milosevic's room for manoeuvre, as he was now faced with a NATO committed to the enforcement of a peace agreement that the Kosovars had signed on to. Still, the Serbian dictator calculated – not entirely incorrectly – that NATO was extremely reluctant to use force, that a use of force would be militarily inconsequential and likely to fracture the alliance, and that the domestic political benefits to be gained from continued operations in Kosovo and defiance of NATO outweighed the risk of NATO actually following through on its threats. Serbian operations in Kosovo intensified, and no agreement was forthcoming from Milosevic.

NATO began the bombing of limited targets inside Kosovo and Serbia on 24 March. The initial assumption was that a few days of relatively light bombing would convince Milosevic of NATO's seriousness, upon realization of which he would return to negotiations with an improved attitude. As the NATO air commander Lieutenant General Michael Short recalls, 'I had been told – I can't tell you how many times – this will all be over in three nights ... I am not personally convinced that all of our leaders had come to grips with the possibility of a prolonged air campaign ... they genuinely thought all NATO had to do was demonstrate resolve'.[13] With this in mind, both President Clinton and Tony Blair appeared to rule out the use of ground troops in their televised addresses at the beginning of the bombing.

Unfortunately, Milosevic's calculations were somewhat different. Judging that the bombing was operationally ineffectual and gave him the persona, in Serbia at least, of being wronged against, he radically increased the pace of ethnic cleansing operations in Kosovo, displacing a significant proportion of the Albanian population and filling Western TV screens with horrific images of refugees and atrocities against civilians. NATO's strategy had failed badly – not only had Milosevic refused to capitulate but the very acts the intervention was designed to halt had been increased exponentially. There could now be no question of a halt to military action, and indeed the alliance was faced with a quite tricky task: to convince a non-plussed Milosevic of its seriousness, having announced that there was no intention to consider the use of on-the-ground forces. The bombing was intensified, and the target set expanded to include the infrastructure of Serbia proper.

However, the initial weeks of the expanded air war were at best unsatisfactory and at times calamitous. Alliance pilots dropped their bombs from high altitude to eliminate the possibility of being shot down, but even the technologically advanced warplanes found it difficult to identify Serbian military targets carrying out operations tens of thousands of feet below in Kosovo. A gruesome illustration of the difficulties came on 14 April, when an air attack on what had initially appeared to be a convoy of Serb troops turned out to be comprised of Kosovo Albanian refugees. This action caused the death of seventy civilians. Much more commonly, however, NATO warplanes would return to base with a full load having failed to identify targets, and the Serb army in Kosovo was able to proceed relatively unimpeded. Attacks on targets inside Serbia proper also failed to do much to sway

Milosevic, and the morality of bombing the 'Serb propaganda machine', which in practice sometimes meant journalists in TV studios, was questioned. David Blunkett's diary records his opinion that at this point, 'efforts in Kosovo [we]re a mess'.[14] Chris Smith, a member of the cabinet at the time, recalls that 'there was nervousness, certainly', in the government:

> There had been some cases where bombs had not found their proper targets, there was the very unfortunate incident of the bombing of the Chinese Embasssy in Belgrade, there seemed to be no lessening of resolve on the part of the Serbs and Milosevic. There was a period when [we wondered] are we actually doing the right thing? Is it producing the right results?[15]

According to Alastair Campbell's diaries, a telephone call between Blair and Clinton on 14 April involved both of them 'hitting the panic buttons quite hard'.[16]

By the end of April, Tony Blair in particular had become convinced that the air campaign was failing, and that NATO was effectively losing the war.[17] He determined that NATO credibility was at stake, that the alliance had a moral duty to prevent the ethnic cleansing from being completed, and that only the introduction of ground troops, or at least the credible threat of such a move, could compel Milosevic to desist. This placed Blair at odds with other NATO governments, and most significantly with much of the Clinton administration and the president himself, distracted by the domestic scandal of the Monica Lewinsky affair. Blair engaged in serious and sustained lobbying of the president, finding an ally in the hawkish secretary of state Madeline Albright, but a degree of anger from the president and his other advisers at his 'grandstanding' and 'over-adrenalized' performance. Other NATO governments either had populations that were strongly opposed to the use of ground troops (Greece and Italy), or were convinced that such a move would fracture the alliance (France and Germany). In this context, Blair took the gamble of raising the rhetoric involved with the war, casting it as a conflict between good and evil, 'civilization and barbarity', promising to the Kosovar refugees directly that they would be allowed to return to their homes, and continuing to push Clinton hard on ground troops. Blair signalled his seriousness in late May with the beginning of preparations for implementing the British army's 'Operation Bravo Minus', which called for an opposed invasion of Kosovo and the commitment of 50,000 British troops – practically the entire deployable strength of the army.[18]

This recommitment to the war effort placed Blair in an exposed position both domestically and internationally, at odds with his allies, and having committed his political future to events over which he was not really in control. NATO as a whole was also presented with a tremendous problem – how to keep the creaking alliance together while applying enough pressure on Milosevic to win the war.

Fortunately for both Blair and for NATO developments that seemed to come right out of the blue saved them from having to make a final decision on the ground troop option. Milosevic signalled his willingness to cease operations in Kosovo. The ultimate cause of Milosevic's capitulation is debatable, but a combination of the withdrawal of Russian diplomatic support, the increasing efficacy of the air campaign and the increasing success of ground operations against Serbian forces by the KLA, and the perception that NATO just might launch a ground invasion, convinced Milosevic to cease operations in Kosovo and concentrate on retaining power in Serbia.

Blair and the war

A realist analysis

Before analysing the impact of Blair's personality on events in Kosovo, we should consider how far an actor-general realist approach can take us in understanding what happened.

A realist would begin with an analysis of the threat posed by Milosevic's activities. Blair did make the case that instability from Kosovar Albanian refugees had the potential to destabilize surrounding countries, with consequences for Europe as a whole. However, this did not rise to the level of imminent or serious threat to British national security, nor did Blair lean heavily upon it in making the case for war. A further realist justification would consider the credibility of NATO as an alliance. If it could not compel a militarily weak Serbia to desist in policies that had been declared unacceptable, what would be the standing of the alliance in future confrontations? This was indeed a case Blair sought to make, and Milosevic had in fact made the calculation that NATO's will was weak.

However, the 'credibility of NATO' explanation, while useful in explaining the dynamics of conflict once the air war had begun, is less helpful in accounting for the initial decision to become involved in the Kosovo crisis – NATO's credibility was not on the line until its leaders, with Blair in the front row, committed themselves to Milosevic's unconditional surrender. Further, the NATO credibility hypothesis would predict that leaders of all NATO countries would be concerned with the credibility of the alliance, and especially, one would suppose, the leader of the major power – the United States. An additional difficulty with the NATO credibility hypothesis as a sufficient explanation, then, is in accounting for Blair's hawkishness on the issue and Clinton's comparative timidity.

Compelling strategic or political reasons for the nature and form of the policies Blair championed do not, therefore, readily present themselves, suggesting that an analysis focused solely upon realist threat calculations is insufficient as an explanation for British actions.[19] A realist perspective does, however, sensitize us to the importance of the United States to any effective NATO policy in the region, and provides context for the effort Blair put into shaping US policy on the issue. Coercive diplomacy against Serbia was effectively impossible for European states acting alone, even given the 'backyard' locale. US airpower constituted the overwhelming majority of available force. Blair's moralism was meaningless absent US power. However, even here a realist analysis encounters some troubling behaviours – especially Blair's aggressive lobbying of the senior ally for a commitment of ground troops and the perception he created in the Clinton administration that they were being publicly embarrassed. The logic, from an alliance maintenance standpoint, of outbidding the senior ally on the side of hawkishness is perhaps slightly cloudy. As Clare Short put it, 'he spun against Clinton which was pretty shocking because he'd positioned himself very strongly to be very friendly with Clinton'.[20]

While a first cut focused upon power and threat is a reasonable base, it does seem that much of the evidence calls for an individual-level analysis. Reflecting upon his policies following the conclusion of the war, Blair maintained that it was his judgment that the conflict was essentially about morality rather than utility, suggesting that it was possible to view the war as:

> an act of self-interest, in the sense that I think had we not intervened in Kosovo there would have been serious consequences for Europe as a whole. But if I'm frank about it, that's not what really motivated me during it ... to allow genocide to happen right on our doorstep and do nothing about it would have been criminal on our part.[21]

Belief in ability to control events

With his high belief in his ability to control events, Blair would be expected to take a proactive foreign policy stance, to believe himself influential over international actors and events, and to hold an optimistic view of the outcome of action. His behaviour during the Kosovo crisis is consistent with these expectations in three major ways.

First, Blair's proactive advocacy of military action against Milosevic, and especially his positioning of himself as by far the greatest NATO enthusiast for ground troops, reflects an internal locus of control. From very early in the crisis, Blair was NATO's chief hawk,[22] suggesting that there was a necessity for action from those with the power to be effective.[23] Blair became convinced not only that action was necessary, but that 'his own leadership was vital'.[24] His proactive stance was most evident on the question of ground troops, the use of which most NATO governments were either reluctant to raise or strongly opposed to. Blair himself judges he 'was always in the forward end of the troupe on this', and indeed his lobbying of Clinton and other NATO governments, and activation of the British army's 'Operation Bravo Minus' plan is evidence to this effect. As the NATO air campaign appeared to be failing in mid-March, Blair displayed optimism and sought to push deeper with an action others were questioning: 'I think it is extremely important to carry on the air campaign and intensify it.' On ground troops, he developed the notion of their being employed into 'a semi-permissive environment', a euphemism for their use in combat rather than as peacekeepers, and refused to echo the ruling out of ground forces by other NATO countries: 'We keep every single option under review.'[25]

More generally, his response to doubters within the cabinet was that the key to victory was to stay 'rock solid' and 'hold our nerve',[26] while he bolstered President Clinton's resolve with the reminder that 'we had started it, and we had to see it through and finish it'.[27] General Wesley Clark, the supreme NATO commander who received Blair in mid-April, reports him 'leaning hard to push ahead for planning the ground option'.[28] General Charles Guthrie, the head of the UK military, recalled that 'the Americans under Clinton were very, very casualty averse … we were much more forward-leaning, and wanted to go in on the ground, and we planned to go in on the ground'. The judgment of Guthrie, which Blair shared, was that 'high-level bombing, week after week, month after month, is not going to work in the end, because mistakes will be made, and people will get fed up with it'.[29]

Indeed, Blair's persistent efforts to secure a commitment of ground forces, and his belief in his ability to persuade President Clinton that this was necessary, are a further reflection of his internal locus of control. A key focus of these efforts was NATO's fiftieth anniversary summit, to be held 22–24 April. In the run up to this summit, which would be dominated by the alliance's faltering progress in its first war, Blair had resolved that ground troops were the only guarantee of victory, and that he would seek to deliver them through persuading Clinton that they were necessary. He wrote to the president forcefully setting out this position,[30] and made public statements of a more hawkish character than the other allies. Blair continued to rely upon his euphemistic formulations of all options being under consideration, and ground forces being used in a 'semi-permissive' environment, a notion that this time drew the tart response from US General Hugh Shelton that he doubted his troops would get 'semi-shot'.

Blair, who had characteristic faith in his ability to persuade the Americans on the ground troop issue, was surprised by how difficult a task this proved to be, and frustrated at the caution of the Americans. The secretary of defense, William Cohen, told Blair that ground troops were an 'almost impossible sell' domestically , while the vice president, Al Gore, was concerned that a commitment would wreck his forthcoming election campaign.[32] The British ambassador to the US, Sir Christopher Meyer, reports that 'the Americans weren't having it. They were unshakeable.'[33] The president himself had received great criticism for launching cruise missile attacks on Iraq, being accused of seeking to distract attention from his ongoing impeachment proceedings. Blair's proactive stance on the issue led to some Clinton advisers dubbing him 'Winston Blair', ready to 'fight to the last American', and needing to 'sprinkle less adrenalin on his cornflakes'.[34]

When Blair met with Clinton prior to the summit, he restated his position. Wesley Clark records that these discussions were 'stormy' and Blair did not temper his stance.[35] Clinton frankly told him to 'pull himself together',[36] and pointed out to Blair the differences in the powers of their jobs and the standing of their respective countries in the world.[37] Clinton himself comments that 'I didn't find the argument that I should pursue a course that would cost more American lives without enhancing the prospects of victory very persuasive'.[38] General Guthrie, accompanying Blair in meetings with the president, felt that Clinton would seem to assent to the use of ground troops, then later be talked out of it by his advisers: 'we felt that Clinton agreed with us. And then, he didn't.'[39]

The danger was that the appearance of disunity would overshadow the NATO summit, and would confirm Milosevic's suspicions that the alliance lacked the internal unity to enforce its will. Indeed, when Blair sought to inject some urgency into the situation by preparing deployment orders for British troops, the move was dismissed by the Italian prime minister as 'a totally useless exercise', while German Chancellor Shroeder refused to 'participate in this specifically British debate on war theory'.[40] The ultimate result of the discussions with Clinton was a very private if ambiguous commitment from the American president to do 'whatever is necessary' to win. The price for this was that Blair was instructed to hold his peace about ground troops during the NATO summit.

More generally, Blair's confidence in his and NATO's efficacy and the ambition and scope of his policies was a defining feature of his conduct during the war. His definition of success for the operation was expansive: the return of the Kosovar refugees, which would necessarily involve a Serbian retreat and NATO occupation of Kosovo. Blair tied not only his own but also NATO's credibility to achieving this objective. If they did not stand firm, Blair argued, then 'the next time ... we say we are going to take action, people would say, well, prove it'.[41] His public promise to the Kosovar refugees he visited at a camp in Albania was 'We will not let you down. We will make sure that you are able to return to your homes, and live in peace.'[42] This was a commitment which other NATO leaders had studiously avoided making, and the chances of its fulfilment were highly uncertain for much of the conflict. Blair's associates worried that the combination of the rupture with allies over ground troops and the public statement of ambitious war aims meant that 'Tony is doing too much, he's overdoing it and he's overplaying his hand.'[43]

The cabinet secretary, Richard Wilson, told Blair frankly that he was putting himself in 'a very dangerous position', and that the conflict could go 'badly wrong'.[44] In fact, General Wesley Clark pulled Blair's close aide Alastair Campbell aside during the visit to Washington to caution him that

> I like you, and I like your prime minister. And you are your prime minister need to be very careful. Because if I hear the noises out of Washington right, I can hear the sound of saws being sharpened. They are preparing to make a deal, and if they make a deal they will cut through the tree and you and your prime minister are going to be stranded on the bit they cut.[45]

His biographers have considered his actions 'an uncalibrated gamble using uncertain means over which he had limited control for an imprecisely defined end'.[46] Blair, as John Rentoul argued, 'could not have been sure whether the NATO alliance would hold – and most importantly whether Clinton would stay the course ... he had no idea whether Clinton ... could be leveraged into a more robust position'.[47] A close adviser noted that by adopting this position, Blair had gambled '[e]verything. The future of NATO and the future of his government both hinge on a successful resolution ... he really has all his eggs in one basket.'[48] The prime minister himself was aware of the risks he was running, confiding to alarmed aides that, at this point, 'it's shit or bust'.[49]

That the gamble ultimately paid off does not diminish its audacity. Blair's belief in his personal efficacy in altering the position of the Americans and the NATO allies on ground troops, his raising of the stakes by publicly defining expansive war aims, and his proactive stance throughout the conflict are behaviours which are consistent with a leader with a high belief in their ability to control events.

Conceptual complexity

As an individual lower in conceptual complexity, we would expect Blair to view the political world in essentially dichotomous terms, perceiving relatively little nuance in the political environment. As discussed in Chapter 3, lower complexity leaders tend to organize the world into straightforward categories ('them and us', 'good and evil'), and be intolerant of ambiguity. They tend to be decisive and dislike reconsidering a course of action once they have committed to it.

Blair's definitive worldview and intolerance of ambiguity decisively shaped Britain's approach to the Kosovo war. First, he framed the issue from the outset not in terms of a strategic necessity to act, but in terms of right and wrong, in so doing employing the binary 'good and evil' categorizations that have often been associated with lower complexity leaders. Blair considered Milosevic as simply a 'bully and a deeply evil man',[50] and suggested that once refugees started pouring out of Kosovo, it was 'no longer just a military conflict. It is a battle between good and evil, between civilization and barbarity', a framing of the situation that was almost 'biblical'.[51] Visiting Kosovar refugees, Blair further raised the stakes: 'This is not a battle for NATO, this is not a battle for territory, this is a battle for humanity.'[52] He talked increasingly in terms of the equivalence of Serbian ethnic cleansing with the racial policies of the Nazis, displaying the characteristic tendency of lower complexity leaders to make surface-level analogical comparisons.[53] Where others saw ambiguity in NATO's somewhat confused stance and aims early in the conflict, Blair argued that they were 'crystal clear'. His address to the British people at the beginning of the conflict expressed this certainty: 'We are doing what is right, for a world that must know that barbarity cannot be allowed to defeat justice. This is, simply, the right thing to do.'[54]

This black-and-white view of the moral stakes involved led Blair to a further behaviour indicative of lower complexity leaders: an unwillingness to consider any compromise or partial settlement. 'There are no half-measures about Milosevic's brutality', he reasoned, so '[t]here can be no half-measures about how we deal with it. No compromise, no fudge, no half-baked deals.'[55] Many of the NATO allies would have found a deal along the lines of previous negotiated settlements of post-Yugoslavia conflicts to be the most sensible course of action, and indeed a close adviser counselled him to consider a negotiated solution. 'If there is going to be a fudge, I'm not going to be part of it', he responded. As part of his advice about Blair's over-exposed position, the cabinet secretary, Richard Wilson, urged him to consider the diplomatic options given Clinton's reticence to commit ground forces:

> It looked as though there was a real danger that President Clinton and the European allies might slither into some sort of fudged formula with Milosevic', he recalled, 'and I said to him I think there's a real risk that you're going to be left out on a limb and you'll find everyone else is in favour of a wording and you're on your own ... what will you do if you find yourself in that position?' And he said 'I will be right, and I will say that I am right and I'm not afraid of standing on my own'. I was struck by that ... certainty, determination, and willpower.[57]

Indeed, Blair was unrelenting: 'We will carry on pounding day after day after day, until our objectives are secured', he stated. 'There can be no compromise whatever with NATO's essential war aims.'[58] The combination of Blair framing the conflict in the highest possible moral terms and his resolute refusal to consider anything short of complete and total victory startled not only allies but also cabinet colleagues, and while the cabinet remained much more unified during this crisis than Blair's subsequent wars, concerns were aroused about his judgment given the almost messianic stance he had adopted.[59]

Need for power

Leaders higher in need for power prefer tightly to control decision-making processes, want to be closely involved in the major aspects of policy making and are reluctant to delegate. These leaders often fashion decision-making processes which involve small groups and interact in relatively informal ways, which can lead to a downgrading of the role of formalized decision structures and bureaucracies.

Blair's behaviour during the Kosovo crisis cemented this style as his favoured approach to foreign policy making. Before the Kosovo situation commanded international attention, Blair was content to allow the foreign secretary, Robin Cook, to handle the intricate diplomatic processes. However, once military action became likely, Blair seized control.[60] He took personal charge and, a senior official reports 'focused single-mindedly on just one issue'.[61] 'He became very engaged', Clare Short comments.[62] His involvement extended to micromanagement of the air campaign, agreeing targets for each night's attacks and closely questioning military officials.[63] The military welcomed Blair's decisiveness, with General Guthrie commenting that 'I thought it was helpful that he made his mind up and gave direction. That's what military people like. They like to be listened to and they like people who make decisions.'[64] The feeling seems to have been mutual, as Blair came to trust the advice he received from military sources and appreciate the operationally minded direction of their analysis, a pattern that would continue throughout the major foreign policy events of his premiership.

This streamlined procedure was extended by Blair to the political aspects of war management. As is characteristic of leaders with a higher need for power, to manage the war Blair created a small, handpicked decision-making group that operated outside of regular bureaucratic structures. John Rentoul reports that this group

> met in his study just after nine on most mornings. Guthrie and the politicians sat on the sofa and armchairs, with the officials in a horseshoe around the edges of the room. Sir Richard Wilson, the Cabinet Secretary, often took the minutes on his knee, perched on the sofa. The informality of style – the Prime Minister sometimes eating an apple during proceedings – belied Blair's firm grasp of decision making.[65]

This does not mean that the cabinet was excluded, and indeed the principles underpinning the war were discussed and accepted largely uncritically by most ministers.[66] However, during the majority of the war, when the outcome was uncertain, Blair did keep a tight rein on both information and decision making, informing the cabinet in only 'irregular and unspecific' terms. At low points, 'a siege mentality seized Blair's immediate entourage'.[67]

His low regard for the formal decision-making procedures of the cabinet extended to frustration with the bureaucratized and cautious advice of the Foreign Office, and he responded to their analyses of the air campaign's failings angrily: 'The establishment! The bloody establishment! What would they have done?'[68] The processes and compromises of alliance and working through international organizations also vexed him. General Guthrie recalls that 'you were not a free agent. Everything had to be argued and talked about and papers submitted and Ambassadors took a view and ministers took a view, and it did feel like a terribly laborious process to him'.[69]

The ultimately successful outcome of the war, in which he had persisted against the advice of many that it was imprudent and he should consider compromise, acted to increase his confidence in both his own judgment and the tightly held decision-making procedures he had employed: 'Very few had shared his sense of certainty: it further increased his reliance on and trust in the small circle around him and increased his suspicions of the Whitehall establishment. It was to this tight-knit group that he would turn again in future foreign crises.'[70]

The Doctrine of the International Community

In the midst of the Kosovo conflict, Blair made the most significant foreign policy speech of his prime ministership. In the United States on 22 April, prior to the NATO summit, Blair addressed the Economic Club of Chicago. His speech, wherein he set out what he termed his 'Doctrine of the International Community', specified principles and justifications for intervention in the world that would apply not only to Kosovo, which Blair stated could not be seen in isolation, but in the subsequent wars in which he involved the United Kingdom. Addressing Kosovo, Blair restated his hawkish position, 'We cannot let the evil of ethnic cleansing stand. We must not rest until it is reversed ... Success is the only exit strategy I am prepared to consider.'[71] In its broader aspects the speech, which displayed a black-and-white view of the world in moral terms and advocated a proactive stance from the western allies, was also a clear reflection of Blair's underlying personality traits.

Blair suggested that wars in the modern international system would be fought not for 'territorial ambitions' but for 'values'.[72] He enunciated five principles for judging the wisdom of a military intervention, which were almost identical to the well-known 'Powell Doctrine': is the case for use of force strong? Has diplomacy been exhausted? Is there a usable military option? Has there been adequate preparation for the aftermath of the use of force? Are national interests involved?

To these somewhat innocuous and vague standards Blair then appended a more radical notion. 'The most pressing foreign policy problem we face', he stated, 'is to identify the circumstances in which we should get involved in other people's conflicts. Non-interference has long been considered an important principle of international order ... But the principle of non-interference must be qualified in important respects.' This was a manifesto for a proactive, muscular approach to international politics, based upon a clear moral imperative for powerful liberal states to intervene in the affairs of non-liberal states on humanitarian grounds. Powerful liberal states not only could, but must, adopt proactive foreign policies: 'just as with the parable of the individuals and the talents, so those nations which have the power have the responsibility.'[73] This was a seminal text, providing not only a rationale for the ongoing intervention in Kosovo but also in some ways prefiguring the later involvement in Iraq. It was a departure from notions of pragmatic realpolitik in its ambition and scope, and the attempt to equate material interests and normative values.[74]

The Doctrine of the International Community is difficult to explain as a product of a strategic or domestic imperative, but does fit quite readily with Blair's individual characteristics as we have identified them. His lower complexity affords him a comfort with clear-cut moral distinctions involving types of states and the absolute justice of some causes versus the absolute injustice of others, and his high belief in his ability to control events predisposes him towards proactive policies, of which the interventionist doctrine of the text promises many. Finally, the provenance of the speech was typically Blairite in being composed by a small number of ad hoc advisers, with intellectual capital coming from London School of Economics professor Lawrence Freedman, and being prepared outside of regularized foreign office channels. Indeed, career diplomats were uneasy at the extensity of commitments the doctrine seemed to imply, and upon learning of the new British foreign policy framework the foreign office had to scramble somewhat to accommodate to it.[75]

What difference did Blair make?

We have seen above good evidence of congruence between the behaviours we would expect of a leader with Blair's worldview and style, and his actual behaviour during the Kosovo war. Can we push the argument a step further and assert that Blair as an individual was causally necessary to British policy and the outcome of the war? Consistent with the logic for assessing the impact of individuals developed in Chapter 2, we can separate this question into two elements: would any British prime minister have acted as Blair did? Would the outcome of the Kosovo war have been different absent Blair's involvement?

Would any prime minister have acted as Blair did? One way to answer this question is to look at different individuals in comparable situations. The previous prime minister, John Major, had in fact proven extremely reluctant to become involved in the post-Yugoslavia situation, counting against the hypothesis that any individual in post at the time would have acted as Blair did. Blair and his close advisers felt that Major's government had suffered a failure of foreign policy nerve in refusing to get involved in Bosnia, and were determined not to reproduce those policies. As one of Blair's key advisers reports: 'Frankly, we were appalled at the cowardice of the Tories.' This adviser also locates the source of the different policies followed by the new Labour government in Blair as an individual: 'It was a moral thing with Tony. He believed very strongly that Britain should be a force for good in the world.'[76] The change in Britain's stance was noted by the US State Department: 'The British no longer had to be dragged along to confront the Serbs', said a senior official. 'We saw a completely different attitude.'[77] Lord Guthrie, who served both Major and Blair, saw a stark difference in their attitudes toward the Balkans: 'When Blair came in, he took a much more forward-leaning role than John Major.' Blair's decisiveness and proactive style found favour with the upper echelons of the armed forces, says Guthrie: 'As far as I'm concerned, he was certainly a much easier prime minister to work for than his predecessor John Major … I tell you what, I did admire some of the decisions he took.'[78]

In some ways, these comparisons of Major and Blair can be seen as a quasi-natural experiment: two leaders facing related situations in the same period of time. Observers and participants agree that Blair was by far the more proactive and decisive of the two.

The question then arises as to the significance of British foreign policy, as shaped by Blair, upon the outcome of the war overall. The most authoritative account of the war, by Ivo Daalder and Michael O'Hanlon of the Brookings Institution, suggests that Blair and Britain were only secondary factors in NATO's success. They suggest that the withdrawal of Russian diplomatic support for Serbia, as well as the slow moves towards the use of decisive force by the USA, played a much greater role in altering Milosevic's calculus than the actions of Britain, a state which was supplying only 4 per cent of NATO's airpower.[79]

However, Blair and his close advisers certainly believe that their bullish leadership, and in particular the progress they thought they had made towards orchestrating preparations for the introduction of ground troops, was extremely significant,[80] David Blunkett, who was dining with Blair on the night Milosevic capitulated, believes the prime minister 'played an absolutely essential role in persuading Bill Clinton that ground troops and direct intervention was necessary'.[81] Sir Jeremy Greenstock judges that 'he was an important adviser to Clinton, if you want to put it that way. His voice was important to Clinton. And I think the evidence is, from the British end at any rate, that Blair stiffened the Americans and kept them going ... He took a risk there, but he was right.'[82]

However, From the American side, the evidence is ambiguous. As a Clinton aide put it, 'Blair's pressure did help steel some of us in the administration, but ultimately his input was merely to speed up what would have happened anyway'.[83] In terms of the difference Blair as an individual made, we do seem to satisfy the condition of actor dispensability. Blair's worldview and style were necessary to the decisions the UK made. In terms of action dispensability, there is also some evidence that Blair made a difference to the outcome, although with the caveat that other factors – the change in course by the Russians and the independent analysis of the Clinton administration, were also key in securing a successful outcome.

Sierra Leone

Blair's involvement in the Kosovo War was echoed just months later by a smaller scale involvement in the former British colony of Sierra Leone. The Sierra Leone episode, while not of the magnitude of Kosovo, Afghanistan, and Iraq, is an important marker in Blair's foreign policy development, displaying the proactive policy stance, stark framing of issues, and increasingly personalistic approach to policy decisions that he had become comfortable with.

Sierra Leone is a former British colony, founded in 1787 partly as a refuge for freed slaves. By the late twentieth century, the country had suffered immensely from civil war and the pathologies of arms and drug smuggling, along with the illicit diamond trade. Various well-armed and deeply unpleasant militias had come to exist that under-mined central government authority, and the most powerful of these – the 'Revolutionary United Front' – achieved in May 1997 the ouster of the democratically elected government, led by Ahmad Tejan Kabbah.

Attempting to regain power - and to quickly create an effective fighting force in order that he might have a chance to retain it - Kabbah purchased arms through a variety of at best semi-legitimate means, including from the British company Sandline. The Foreign Office had given approval to Sandline's operations, but they did contravene a UN arms embargo and so came to the attention of another agency of the UK government, Customs & Excise. Causing further embarrassment, the UN embargo in question had originally been imposed by a Security Council resolution drafted by the British. The foreign secretary, Robin Cook, struggled to explain quite how the situation had come about. Blair, however, took control and character-istically framed the episode in terms of moral absolutes. The arms, along with help from neighbouring Nigeria, had enabled Kabbah to retake power and the subsequent entry of a large UN peacekeeping force had stabilized the country. Therefore, the 'good guys' won: 'Don't let us forget that what was happening was that the UN and the UK were both trying to help the democratic regime restore its position from an illegal military coup. They were quite right in trying to do it.'[84]

Instability remained endemic, however, and in May 2000 the Blair government received intelligence that the capital, Freetown, was about to fall once again. Blair took the decision to rapidly deploy 700 British troops in order to carry out a narrowly defined mission of evacuating foreign nationals. With the situation rapidly deteriorating, Blair took a huge gamble. He allowed the UK troops to remain in the capital even though the original mission had been fulfilled, and to take a more active role in bolstering the UN force and the government of Kabbah. The instruction from Blair was to be proactive and follow the more ambitious course of action: 'Go for the radical option.'[85] This turned out to be a success, although nearly with a heavy price tag as a dangerous militia group, the 'West Side Boys', managed to capture as hostages eleven soldiers from the British force.

Blair was told by General Guthrie that any rescue mission would be extremely risky. Again, he was ready to commit to the use of force, and ordered on 10 September a successful raid to recover the soldiers with a force of 150 paratroopers. 'He was outstanding in Sierra Leone', Guthrie recalls:

> He wanted us to act independently [of the UN], and thank heavens he did, because we were able to get on with it ... There were political traps, people saying don't do it, it'll be dangerous, you'll get into trouble, if it goes wrong it'll be ghastly, but he had the guts to go and do it. It was certainly very brave.[86]

Sierra Leone again displayed and reinforced key aspects of the Blair style. The issue was framed in terms of moral absolutes, the more ambitious and proactive policy option was chosen, and Blair took personal control of decision making once a crisis had developed. In tandem with the successful intervention in Kosovo, Sierra Leone gave Blair increased confidence in his foreign policy judgment and efficacy.[87] As Blair left office in 2007, he remained a heroic figure in Sierra Leone, feted on a farewell tour as a saviour of sorts and being presented with child after child named after him.

Conclusion

Kosovo and Sierra Leone represent significant episodes in Blair's development as a foreign policy decision maker. His style of setting ambitious goals, proactively pursued, and based upon the stark framing of issues, led him in these episodes into exposed positions that constituted gambles over events he did not control. He committed British forces, backing his own judgment against that of others, and was successful. The head of the British army, Sir Mike Jackson, comments that 'When you've had that experience of doing it once, you can draw on that experience and it gives you confidence, if you have to, to do it a second or third time'.[88] David Blunkett notes that 'he hadn't wavered, even when people had been saying that it was hopeless and that we would never succeed'.[89]

The successful resolution of the conflict therefore strengthened Blair in the foreign policy style he had adopted, and represents also the highpoint of his 'doctrine of the international community'. Blair learned additional lessons from Kosovo that would be extremely significant in future crises. United Nations support, he discovered, while having huge ability to legitimize foreign policy actions for the domestic British audience, could not be considered a prerequisite for taking action, and its imprimatur was not ultimately necessary in order to get things done.[90] Blair would later note the irony that many who encouraged him to intervene in Kosovo on human rights grounds despite the absence of UN approval would subsequently condemn him for intervening in Iraq – a future occasion where explicit authorization could not be obtained.[91] Chris Smith, a cabinet minister supportive of the Kosovo decisions but who would break with Blair over Iraq, judges that

> [T]he success that he had in Kosovo led directly to the almost hubris that he had over Iraq, the sense that 'I can defy the world and be proved right', the sense that 'I don't need the United Nations to give me authorization', that 'I'm on a crusade, I can change the world and I'm going to do it by sheer will and determination'. That sense that he got about Kosovo led him into a huge trap when it came to Iraq.[92]

Blair also drew a key conclusion from his rebuke by Clinton over the public proselytizing for the introduction of ground troops. Criticizing the United States in public, Blair determined, was ineffective and had the potential to damage British standing with its spectacularly powerful alliance partner. It was crucial to retain influence with the Americans because absent their engagement, Blair's proactive policies and stark moralism would be exercises in empty rhetoric. Future attempts to influence policy would be private, he decided, and the public face would be one of absolute unity.[93] Indeed, Blair took to heart advice Clinton gave him during the last days of his presidency: 'Don't let your friendship with America wane just because I'm gone.'[94]

Notes

1 A. Rawnsley, *Servants of the People* (London: Hamish Hamilton, 2000), p. 274.
2 C. Coughlin, *American Ally* (New York: HarperCollins, 2006). p. 98.
3 M. Walker and I. Black, 'Hawkish Britain ruffles NATO allies', *The Guardian*, 18 May 1999, p. 1.
4 J. Kampfner, *Blair's Wars* (London: Simon and Schuster, 2004), p. 36.
5 A. Seldon, *Blair* (London: Free Press, 2004), p. 385.
6 A. Rawnsley, 'Peace and war', *Observer*, 8 April 2007. Available at http://observer.guardian.co.uk/blair/story/0,,2049947,00.html accessed 8 April 2007.

7 *Frontline*, interview with John Rentoul, 21 March 2003. Available at www.pbs.org/wgbh/pages/frontline/shows/blair/prime/rentoul.html, accessed 7 April 2007.

8 Author interview with Clare Short, 30 April 2007.

9 Author interview with David Blunkett, 1 May 2007.

10 J. Naughtie, *The Accidental American: Tony Blair and the Presidency* (New York: Public Affairs, 2004), p. 51.

11 The body set up by Britain, France, Germany, Italy, Russia and the US during the Bosnia war, and which remained active in monitoring developments in the Balkans.

12 M. Albright, *Madame Secretary: A Memoir* (New York: Miramax, 2006), p. 405.

13 R. Vickers, 'Blair's Kosovo campaign: political communications, the battle for public opinion and foreign policy', *Civil Wars,* 3:1 (2000), 57.

14 D. Blunkett, *The Blunkett Tapes: My Life in the Bear Pit* (London: Bloomsbury, 2006), p. 121.

15 Author interview with Chris Smith, 18 June 2007.

16 A. Campbell, The Blair Years (New York: Knopf, 2007), p. 376.

17 P. Stephens, *Tony Blair: The Making of a World Leader* (New York: Viking, 2004), p. 155.

18 Rawnsley, *Servants of the People*, p. 286.

19 See L. Richardson, 'A force for good in the world? Britain's role in the Kosovo crisis', in P. Martin and M. R. Brawley (eds), *Allied Force or Forced Allies? Alliance Politics, Kosovo, and NATO's War* (New York: Palgrave, 2000) for a similar line of reasoning.

20 Author interview with Clare Short, 30 April 2007.

21 Coughlin, *American Ally*, p. 106.

22 R. N.-Taylor, 'The Kosovo crisis: going to war?', *The Guardian*, 9 October 1998, p. 5.

23 J. Rentoul, *Tony Blair, Prime Minister* (London: Warner Books, 2001), p. 509.

24 Seldon, *Blair*, p. 394.

25 D. Auersweld, 'Explaining wars of choice: an integrated decision model of NATO policy in Kosovo', *International Studies Quarterly*, 48:3 (2004), 648.

26 P. Riddell, *Hug Them Close: Blair, Clinton, Bush and the 'Special Relationship'* (London: Politico's, 2003), p. 107.

27 Vickers, 'Blair's Kosovo Campaign', p. 66.

28 W. Clark, Waging Modern War: Bosnia, Kosovo, and the Future of Combat, (New York: Public Affairs, 2001), p. 264.

29 Interview with General Guthrie, 6/20/07.

30 Seldon, Blair, p. 386.

31 Kampfner, Blair's Wars, p. 47.

32 Vickers, 'Blair's Kosovo campaign', p. 66.

33 BBC Television, *Blair: The Inside Story* (part two). Airdate: Tuesday 27 February 2007.

34 Riddell, *Hug Them Close*, p. 108.

35 Clark, *Waging Modern War*, p. 268.

36 Kampfner, *Blair's Wars*, p. 57.

37 Naughtie, *The Accidental American*, p. 50.
38 W. J. Clinton, *My Life* (New York: Random House, 2004), p. 851.
39 Author interview with Lord Guthrie, 20 June 2007.
40 Richardson, 'A force for good in the world', p. 148.
41 Ibid., p. 152.
42 Rawnsley, *Servants of the People*, p. 263.
43 Kampfner, *Blair's Wars*, p. 49.
44 Rawnsley, *Servants of the People*, p. 281.
45 Campbell, *The Blair Years*, p. 385.
46 Rawnsley, *Servants of the People*, p. 258.
47 Rentoul, *Tony Blair, Prime Minister*, p. 525.
48 *Financial Times*, 22 April 1999, p. 8.
49 Rawnsley, 'Peace and war'.
50 Seldon, *Blair*, p. 392.
51 Kampfner, *Blair's Wars*, p. 57.
52 Kampfner, *Blair's Wars*, p. 54.
53 See S. B. Dyson and T. Preston, 'Individual characteristics of political leaders and the use of analogy in foreign policy decision making', *Political Psychology*, 27:6 (2006), 249–72.
54 BBC Television, *Blair: The Inside Story*.
55 Rawnsley, *Servants of the People*, p. 283; Stephens, *Tony Blair*, p. 160.
56 Coughlin, *American Ally*, p. 83.
57 BBC Television, *Blair: The Inside Story*.
58 M. Walker, I. Traynor and M. White, 'War in Europe: air attacks will be stepped up, says prime minister', *The Guardian*, 13 April 1999, p. 1.
59 Seldon, *Blair*, p. 401.
60 Author interview with Clare Short, 30 April 2007.
61 Seldon, *Blair*, p. 394.
62 Author interview with Clare Short, 30 April 2007.
63 Coughlin, *American Ally*, p.85.
64 Rentoul, *Tony Blair*, p. 522.
65 Ibid., p. 522.
66 Seldon, *Blair*, p. 395.
67 Rawnsley, *Servants of the People*, p. 283.
68 Ibid., p. 283.
69 Interview with Lord Guthrie, 20 June 2007.
70 Seldon, *Blair*, p. 407.
71 T. Blair, 'The Doctrine of the International Community'. Available at www.number10.gov.uk/output/Page1297.asp, accessed 20 May 2007.
72 Ibid.
73 Ibid.
74 T. Dunne, 'Fighting for Values': Atlanticism, internationalism and the Blair doctrine'. Paper presented at the Annual Meetings of the International Studies Association, Honolulu, HI, 1–5 March 2005.
75 Seldon, *Blair*, p. 399; Naughtie, *The Accidental American*, p. 52.
76 Coughlin, *American Ally*, p. 76.
77 Seldon, *Blair*, p. 393.
78 Author interview with Lord Guthrie, 20 June 2007.

79 I. Daalder and M. O'Hanlon, *Winning Ugly: NATO's War to Save Kosovo* (Washington, DC: Brookings Institution Press, 2000), p. 164.
80 Coughlin, *American Ally*, p, 104; Naughtie, *The Accidental American*, p. 51.
81 Author interview with David Blunkett, 1 May 2007.
82 Author interview with Sir Jeremy Greenstock, 6 June 2007.
83 Seldon, *Blair*, p. 403.
84 Kampfner, *Blair's Wars*, p. 68.
85 Ibid., p. 71.
86 Author interview with Lord Guthrie, 20 June 2007.
87 Rentoul, *Tony Blair*, p. 426.
88 BBC Television, *Blair: The Inside Story.*
89 Blunkett, *My Life in the Bear Pit*, p. 126.
90 Coughlin, *American Ally*, p. 159.
91 D. Coates and J. Krieger, *Blair's War* (Cambridge: Polity, 2004), p. 21.
92 Author interview with Chris Smith, 18 June 2007.
93 Coughlin, *American Ally*, pp. 126–7.
94 Kampfner, *Blair's Wars*, p. 73.

5 September 11 and the 'war on terror'

Tony Blair's response to the September 11 2001 attacks was one of unequivocal support for the United States, a framing of the situation in stark terms of good and evil, and elucidation of an ambitiously proactive foreign policy programme to prevent the re-occurrence of attacks of such magnitude. It was therefore quite consistent with the policy style rooted in Blair's personality traits that had crystallized during the Kosovo war. The period following September 11 saw the prime minister, with his foreign policy approach set, fully engaged on the world stage. He sought simultaneously to rally international support for the US whilst ensurng that the American response was a judicious one. The results did not, however, match his aims, and international support ebbed as concern over the scope and aggression of the US response mounted. Blair's basic strategy was in many ways a rational one of supporting the most powerful state in the system after it had been attacked, yet his instinct to be close to the US during this period sowed the seeds of the disastrous Iraq decisions.

September 11 and the Afghanistan war

After the 2000 election, Blair was faced with what seemed to be a particularly difficult problem – whilst he had formed an extremely close relationship with Bill Clinton, his successor George W. Bush was an unknown personally, and there seemed to be little ideological common ground between the two. However, Clinton had counselled Blair to forge a relationship with the new president: 'be his best friend.' Blair, sensitive to the realities of the US-UK alliance and of the centrality of US power to progress in international affairs, needed little encouragement. The first meeting of the two leaders, at Camp David in February 2001, was a success, with Blair adopting the informality he had been told the president appreciated and in turn professing to enjoy Bush's straightforward style. The British were also impressed with the calibre of Bush's appointments to the key foreign policy posts, with heavyweights such as Colin Powell, Donald Rumsfeld, and Dick Cheney on board.[1]

However, the worldview of the new administration did not initially seem to align with that of the Blair government. The Bush administration sought to avoid involving the United States in ambitious multilateral ventures, refusing to sign the Kyoto accord on climate change or become associated with the International Criminal Court. Eyebrows were also raised internationally concerning the president's plans for national missile defence and the abrogation of the 1973 Anti-Ballistic Missile Treaty with Russia that this would necessitate, although Blair gained early some capital with the Bush administration by supporting this move and offering to host part of the infrastructure for the putative missile defence system within the United Kingdom. The pre-9/11 months had thus been a mixed bag. Blair had succeeded in forming a personal relationship with Bush, but there were concerns about the 'sharp elbows' the administration had shown in dealing with some international issues.

When word reached the prime minister, about to address the Trades Union Congress, of the September 11 attacks, he was therefore immediately apprehensive about the US response: 'How is Bush going to react? What will he do?' he asked. In particular, Blair feared that an administration with pre-existing unilateralist instincts would react to the attacks with a display of unrestrained force and act outside of the architecture of the international community. The key danger, Blair said privately, was that the US would simply 'jump out of the international system'.[2] Indeed, Blair may have been even more concerned had he known of a conversation on 12 September between the secretary of defense, Donald Rumsfeld, and the president. On being told there were legal considerations bearing upon a military response to the attacks, Bush responded 'I don't care what the international lawyer says. We are going to kick some ass.'[3]

Among Bush's advisers, the deputy secretary of defense, Paul Wolfowitz, was advocating a broad-based and ambitious response immediately following the attacks: 'The idea that we could live with another 20 years of stagnation in the Middle East that breeds this radicalism and breeds terrorism is, I think, just unacceptable – especially after September 11th. We cannot go back to business as usual.'[4] Indeed, some within the administration immediately raised the issue of whether the time was right to deal with the old problem of Iraq as part of a comprehensive response, regardless of the actual provenance of the attacks. Wolfowitz confirmed that there was a major debate among the administration's foreign policy team at Camp David on 15 September:

> There was a long discussion during the day about what place if any Iraq should have in a counterterrorist strategy. There seemed to be a kind of agreement that yes it should be, but the disagreement was whether it should be in the immediate response or whether you should concentrate simply on Afghanistan first.[5]

Meanwhile, Blair was framing his own response. The United States had to be convinced that other countries supported them, and were ready to offer practical help. In this way, the superpower could be reassured that existing norms, institutions, and alliances offered an effective way of responding to the attacks. A key Blair aide recalls that:.

> From the day of the attack, the prime minister was quite emphatic about what he wanted to do. He was determined that the US must not feel that it was on its own, and that it had friends that would stand by it. We were well aware that how America responded to these attacks would define its relations with the rest of the world, and Blair believed that it was crucial that we were part of that decision-making process.[6]

In the judgment of Peter Riddell, Blair's fears that the US would over-react 'dominated his thinking and behaviour' over the entire period from 9/11 to the Iraq war.[7] As David Blunkett reports, Blair said to him that 'if he hadn't embraced the US and been really positive, they wouldn't have taken any notice of us at all and at least they are doing so now'.[8]

Blair resolved to use this perceived influence in service of two goals. The first and immediate goal was to ensure that the military response of the Bush administration was judicious, well-targeted, and multilateral. Concurrently, Blair sought to ensure that the US stayed engaged with international processes, and to shape this engagement toward a solution of what Blair saw as the root cause of the terrorism problem: the Israel-Palestine issue.[9]

In service of the initial goal, Blair sought to impress upon Bush the need to concentrate on the perpetrators of the attacks – Al Qaeda and their Taliban sponsors, rather than follow the advice of some in his administration to seek a quick confrontation with Iraq. Blair was relieved, on being able to speak to the president the day following the attacks, to hear that the US was not going to lash out indiscriminately: 'I don't want to put a million-dollar missile on a five-dollar tent', Bush told Blair.[10] Blair followed up on this conversation by writing to Bush with advice to concentrate on Afghanistan, give the Taliban an ultimatum, and document for world opinion the evidence that the attacks were the work of Al Qaeda. A precipitate attack on Iraq, Blair wrote, would risk fracturing the strong international sympathy for the United States.

The prime minister was reassured once more when, on his first post-9/11 visit to Washington, Bush pulled him aside and made clear that Afghanistan was the immediate objective: 'Iraq we keep for another day.' The 9/11 commission reported that 'When Blair asked about Iraq, the president replied that Iraq was not the immediate problem. Some members of his administration, he commented, had expressed a different view, but he was the one responsible for making the decisions.'[11] During this visit, Blair impressed the practically-minded president with his desire to get involved. The British, he told Rumsfeld, 'really want to participate. Give them a role.'[12]

Satisfied that the United States was planning a proportionate and judicious response, Blair sought to rally the maximum possible international support for the coming war in Afghanistan. The prime minister launched himself off to an astounding variety of places in the weeks following the attacks, including Washington, Berlin, Paris, New York, Russia, Pakistan, Syria, Saudi Arabia, Israel and Gaza. In eight weeks, according to Riddell, the prime minister had fifty-four meetings with world leaders, travelled on thirty-one flights, and logged more than 40,000 miles.[13] Blair was operating as a 'kind of supra-American secretary of state'[14] or Bush's 'Ambassador at Large'.[15] Aides saw him during this period as 'a man possessed',[16] while cabinet colleague David Blunkett recorded in his diary that 'I fear Tony is killing himself. He went to Saudi Arabia, to Jordan, to Israel and next week he is going to Washington. He's just completely doing himself in – it's frightening.'[17] A Number 10 aide complained that 'just getting meetings into his diary for domestic policy was a great struggle after 9/11'.[18] The Bush administration was happy to accept Blair's help, as the prime minister was an eloquent spokesman internationally and reliable on the issues: 'Blair had both the stature and the contacts to do the diplomacy', a White House official commented, 'He was the only world leader we could trust to do that'.[19]

However, Blair did not encounter overwhelming success on these trips, and his evangelizing on the United States' behalf was seen among European states in particular as slightly puzzling, especially as the Bush administration had been somewhat blunt in rejecting offers of help, including commitments of troops for the Afghanistan operations, from several countries. Indeed, the historical significance of NATO's invocation of its Article 5 common defence clause for the first time was somewhat spoiled when the Bush administration said, in effect, 'don't call us, we'll call you'. The preponderance of senior members of the Bush administration were by instinct unilateralist, and these preferences were reinforced by advice from senior military figures involved in the Kosovo intervention, with the received wisdom being that NATO's cumbersome procedures had hindered the effective projection of United States power.[20] This had been bad enough during Kosovo, but the response to a direct attack on American soil was not going to be subject to international negotiation and veto.

The subsequent war in Afghanistan, then, was by choice waged almost solely by US forces, with Britain pledging troops in back-up roles and contributing marginally through sea-launched cruise missiles. Offers of help from other NATO countries were effectively ignored. The fighting itself progressed through three phases: an air bombardment beginning Sunday 7 October 2001; a land campaign waged by the local anti-Taliban opposition with US air and special forces support, which gained success with the fall of the major cities of Mazaar-i-sharif (10 November) and the capital Kabul (13 November); and a final campaign in unsuccessful pursuit of Al Qaeda leaders, including Osama bin Laden, in the cave complex of Tora Bora in December.

The campaign against the Taliban, waged by US special forces in coordination with the Afghan 'Northern Alliance' grouping, was highly successful, and taken as evidence for the efficacy of a war-fighting doctrine based around high technology and low troop numbers. However, in a premonition of future difficulties in Iraq, the lack of troop numbers allowed Osama bin Laden, ostensibly the focus of the war, to evade capture.

Blair and the war

A realist analysis

In the remainder of this chapter, I again consider the extent to which Blair's worldview and leadership style shaped his actions, beginning by considering how far an actor-general realist account can take us. A realist approach fares well in relation to some of the major issues of the US-UK relationship during this period. First of all, from a realist standpoint, the positive nature of the relationship Blair forged with Bush is not really a puzzle at all. For realists, ideology is essentially made subordinate to power considerations when the two come into conflict. It is massively in British interests to maintain the alliance with the United States from a pure power politics standpoint. In the lead-up to the first meeting of the two in February 2001, the British were much more nervous than the Americans, in large measure because they had much more at stake. A close aide to Blair, when asked why the prime minister got along so well with the president, explains that 'the starting point is he had to'.[21]

A realist analysis is again an important baseline for understanding Blair's response to 9/11. The major power in the system had been attacked, and was certain to respond militarily. The hegemon in a unipolar system operates with minimal direct constraints, such as are provided in a bi- or multipolar system by the other great powers. The danger, therefore, is that a hegemon provoked may lash out indiscriminately.

Blair perceived this basic structural feature of the post 9/11 situation.[22] Absent his attempts to ingratiate himself with the administration the Bush foreign policy, he believed, would have been 'cruder, more dangerous, and much more unpalatable to those who were now telling him that he should never have become involved as a partner'.[23] Further, the security of the United Kingdom had long been based upon an international order the essentials of which were guaranteed by American power, and in which the UK occupied the role of close friend. If the United States, out of shock, panic, or desire for retribution, were to slip into an entirely unilateralist foreign policy lacking any sense of restraint, British interests would be imperilled. 'When you look back', said a Blair aide in reference to the British response, 'it was the obvious thing to do'.[24]

More than this, Blair also perceived the threat from failed states, and the potential for terrorist groups to operate out of them, to be real and significant. Blair had, in fact, been concerned about the potential threat before 9/11. Sir Jeremy Greenstock reports that Blair had 'asked the British machine to start looking at how we could constrain the Taliban, a good six months before 9/11'. Blair was 'ahead of anyone else in the British system for spotting, or identifying, Afghanistan as a source of threat for UK interests, and wanted to do something about it'.[25] There was, therefore, a compelling security rationale for supporting the United States in its action against Afghanistan. David Blunkett, who as home secretary was responsible for the security of the British Isles, confirms that 'we believed we were as much at risk from global terrorism as the US'.[26]

As Blair reasoned: 'If [terrorism] is the threat of the 21st century, Britain should be in there helping to confront it, not because we are America's poodle, but because dealing with it will make Britain safer'.[27] Not only is it in Britain's interests to remove this threat, but by offering unconditional support 'Blair hopes and expects that in a time of British need the USA would remember and reciprocate'.[28] Indeed, the discoveries following the war of Al Qaeda documents showing attempts to acquire weopons of mass destruction (WMD) strengthened Blair in the belief that the threat was real. An aide comments that:

> here was tangible proof of what Blair had feared all along. It was an example of what he genuinely feared. If a terrorist group successfully got hold of WMD, the consequences were unthinkable. This was not something that had been dreamed up. It was a very real threat. Here it was, and Blair felt very strongly that we had to deal with it. He saw it as one of the great contemporary challenges.[29]

Realist power politics therefore provides a strong baseline explanation of British behaviour during this period. As Azubuike insightfully asks: 'would Blair have taken on the role of a roving ambassador for justice, and committed British financial, human, and military resources to the extent that he had, if the September 11 attacks had been against, say, Brazil or Japan – two other capitalist democracies and Western allies?'[30]

Where a realist approach is less convincing is in explaining the readiness of Blair to embrace the framing of the conflict in absolutist, moral terms, as a long-lasting 'war on terror' that lent strongly on military solutions. Further, the scope and ambition of Blair's policy agenda in response to the September attacks is also difficult to explain from a purely realist basis. Analysis of Blair's personality and worldview can again shed light on these issues.

Belief in ability to control events

As we have seen, Blair's high belief in his ability to control events predisposes him toward a feeling of efficacy in foreign policy, and a proactive policy stance with the delineation of ambitious goals. This factor is a crucial element of Blair's response to 9/11. Speaking to the

Labour party conference three weeks after the attacks on the United States, Blair talked in incredibly broad terms of the opportunities presented for fundamental change in international affairs: 'This is a moment to seize. The kaleidoscope has been shaken. The pieces are in flux. Soon they will settle again, before they do, let us re-order this world around us.' .

Indeed, Blair had an ambitious plan for such a re-ordering, setting out a comprehensive analysis of the root causes of terrorism and failed states in 'the starving, the wretched, the dispossessed, the ignorant, those living in want and squalor from the deserts of Northern Africa to the slums of Gaza, to the mountain ranges of Afghanistan'. These problems could be solved so that 'people everywhere can see the chance of a better future through hard work and the creative power of the free citizen, not the violence and savagery of the fanatic'.[31] This was a highly ambitious agenda, which Matthew D'Ancona describes as 'fantastically grandiose'[32] and James Naughtie reports was 'too much for even the most starry-eyed diplomat-evangelist'.[33] The fear among colleagues was that Blair 'seemed almost to be promising to solve all of the world's problems'.[34] Clare Short writes that 'he had been searching for his legacy. After September 11, he seemed to have found his cause.'[35]

Blair responded that 'some say it's utopian; others that it's dangerous to think that we can resolve all these problems by ourselves … [but] the fact that we can't solve everything doesn't mean that we try to solve nothing. What is clear is that 11 September has not just given impetus and urgency to such solutions, it has opened the world up.'[36] From the standpoint of Blair's personality, the significance of this is not the inherent desirability of the goals, but rather the scope of ambition entailed and perceived command over events they reflect.

Blair's desire to be close to the United States, seeking to act as wise counsellor on world affairs to the inexperienced president, was however somewhat rebuffed by the Bush administration. Blair's efforts to rally support for the US around the world were useful to the US and saved the Bush administration the trouble of having to do so them-selves, but there was little desire to accept troops from NATO coun-tries, or more particularly to accept the more consultative decision processes that would accompany them. Even British special forces, available to help in the capture of Bin Laden during the crucial battles at Tora Bora, were declined permission to do so. A Whitehall official commented at the end of September 2001 that, in terms of the 'war on terror', 'We don't have an exit strategy. And we don't have an entry strategy either.' Seeking to be a full partner with the United States, Blair had 'raised expectations that cannot be fulfilled'.[37] The 'war on terror' was very much an American operation. Blunkett's notes of a 'war cabinet' meeting during this period confirm that 'there was no coordinated strategy between the US and Britain'.[38] Geoff Hoon, the minister of defence, reports feeling that it was 'the American's show'.[39]

In the effort to gain allies for the United States, Blair had attempted some audacious diplomatic manoeuvres, in particular seeking to rally support for the war in Afghanistan in Syria, Saudi Arabia, Jordan, and Gaza. However, these efforts turned into a diplomatic disaster, with Blair gaining little in Riyadh and Jordan, and with Syria's President Assad hijacking their joint press conference to lecture Blair on Middle Eastern politics, describe the Palestinians as freedom fighters against Israel, and denounce the bombing of innocents in Afghanistan.[40] Fellow members of the European Union saw these as puzzling attempts at unilateral diplomacy, since the UK has very little influence in the contemporary Middle East outside of EU channels.

In many ways, Blair was 'staking his own reputation on decisions taken in Washington', a risk he justified by his belief in his personal efficacy in influencing the actions of the United States and of other states in the international system.[41] Blair had started .

> travelling around the world talking to everyone at a very high level and everyone approved of him and it was his high point. He was a global player, everyone was on his side, and I think it sort of went to his head. And he went a bit sort of crazy thinking 'I can be such a big player, I can be the biggest person dealing with the United States of America.'[42]

In these actions can be seen a pattern associated with individuals who score highly in the belief in ability to control events – a proactive policy stance, ambitious and expansive agenda, and the danger of overestimation of influence and degree of control over specific others and events in general.

Conceptual complexity

Blair's lower conceptual complexity strongly shaped his policy response in the period following 9/11 in two key ways: his framing of the situation as one of evil and involving war, when many around him were uncomfortable with such language, and his certainty and conviction about how to react.

Blair's immediate response on the day of 9/11 was couched in heavily moralistic terms: 'This mass terrorism is the new evil in our world today.'[43] His message to President Bush on 12 September was again couched in terms of dealing with 'evil in all its aspects'.[44] Consistent with the tendency of lower complexity individuals to view the world in absolutist categories, Blair stated that the conflict was 'not a battle between the United States of America and terrorism, but between the free and democratic world and terrorism ... we, like them, will not rest until this evil is driven from the world'.[45] Further, Blair was quick to describe the situation as one of war, suggesting on 16 September that 'Whatever the technical or legal issues about a declaration of war, the fact of the matter is that we are at war with terrorism', a war which would be not limited but 'systematic' and aimed at 'the whole machinery of terrorism'.[46] There could be 'no diplomacy with bin Laden or the Taliban regime'. The choice, when faced with terrorism of this sort, was very simple: 'Defeat it, or be defeated by it. And defeat it we must.'[47] 'What galvanized me', he would later say, 'was that it was a declaration of war by religious fanatics who were prepared to wage war without limit. They killed 3,000. But if they could have killed 30,000 or 300,000 they would have rejoiced in it.'[48] In the post-9/11 era, Blair has been consistent in arguing, 'We do face a global struggle between this terrorism based on perversion of the true faith of Islam and the forces of progress ... across the whole of the region'.[49]

This placed Blair very close to the framing of the situation adopted by President Bush, but somewhat out of line with sentiment among cabinet colleagues and other European leaders. Indeed, Bush's famous line in his 20 September 2001 address to the US congress that 'either you are with us or you are with the terrorists' was greeted somewhat nervously in the UK for the simplification of what was seen as a complex picture. Clare Short wrote in her diary that 'All of us were horrified by the events of September 11 but most decent people are very worried by the bellicose statements from Bush and fearful of the US lashing out and killing lots of innocent Afghans and making things worse'.[50] However, Blair's reaction was that he was 'delighted to hear that he [Bush] was going to give such an unequivocal statement'.[51]

Charles Powell, the former foreign affairs adviser to Margaret Thatcher, commented that 'I think it is true to say that President Bush and Prime Minister Blair do share a certain moral certainty about the way the world is going',[52] while Naughtie suggests that 'the difference between Blair and some of those advising him was that he found the "good and evil" rhetoric less scary than they did … No British prime minister has been so willing to use the word *evil* since the defeat of the Nazis sixty years earlier'.[53] Indeed, when asked the seemingly tendentious question as to why he seems to have 'an apocalyptic vision of Armageddon' post-9/11, Blair responded that:.

> I believe there is a serious risk of that and I believe the risk is not a risk that you can run. In other words, I am not saying for a certainty that it will happen, but I am saying that the risk is sufficiently serious that the balance of risks tilts you towards acting and not waiting till it happens.

As Naughtie notes, the acceptance of terms such as Armageddon is unusual in discussions by statesmen of contemporary international affairs.[54]

The second key way in which Blair's lower complexity seems to have shaped his policy response to 9/11 is in the certainty with which he viewed events. Blair suggested that 'Sometimes things happen in politics, an event that is so cataclysmic that, in a curious way, all the doubt is removed. You are very certain as to what has to be said and done. From the outset, I really felt a great sense of that certainty.'[55] The cabinet secretary, Richard Wilson, noted he 'developed a new certainty about his own role, which was really quite remarkable. He gave out a sense of having truly found himself'[56] and showed 'not a flicker of doubt'.[57] For Blair, the issues engaged by terrorism were quite straightforward: 'There is no compromise possible with such people, no meeting of minds … just a choice: defeat it or be defeated by it. And defeat it we must.'[58] Again, this was language and a framing of events that placed Blair much closer to the Bush administration than to most of his colleagues. There was a feeling in the UK, given the long experience of terrorism through the troubles in Ireland, that perhaps talking in terms of military victory and defeat rather over-simplified the nature of the terrorism problem.

Need for power

In the period following 9/11, Blair's high need for power again found expression in a directive, tightly held policy-making process, involving a close circle of advisers and the circumvention of regularized institutions of decision making such as the cabinet and the Foreign Office. This, of course, was a foreign policy decision-making style Blair had grown comfortable with during the Kosovo conflict, and it was quickly replicated in the aftermath of the September 11 attacks.

In the period following 9/11 and into the Afghanistan war, Blair operated primarily through a small inner-circle, dominated by his chief of staff, Jonathon Powell, and media adviser Alastair Campbell, and meeting in his office 'den' several times a day. This group would be briefed directly on the Taliban and Al Qaeda by a similarly small group of intelligence officials.[59] In response to criticism that this was too opaque a process, Blair created a seven member 'war cabinet', but real authority remained concentrated in the inner-circle.[60] The full cabinet met twice in the weeks following 9/11, but these sessions were essentially devoid of debate and Blair tended during them to inform more than consult colleagues. Labour party MPs complained that he 'failed to consult widely enough', and showed 'an impatient disregard for established institutions and procedures in Westminster and Whitehall in his haste to get things done'.[61] In the period after September 11 he acted as 'his own foreign secretary, and his own defence secretary too'.[62] Coughlin judges that by this time, Blair's governing style had become 'almost presidential'.[63]

Blair's high need for power has been linked to the extremely close relationship he formed with President Bush during this period. Indeed, part of the attraction of trans-Atlantic diplomacy for Blair was its directness. As Naughtie explains 'A prime minister and a president can make agreements that stick. They are unlikely to be unscrambled by officials back in the office. Indeed, Blair's attraction to the relationship with Washington was increased by his enjoyment of doing business in this way.'[64] As Clare Short notes, 'he pushed the Foreign Office away and started to concentrate power in Number 10, and when he got closer to the Bush administration he was on the phone, his special adviser talking to Condi Rice, he being the politician in the world who could pick up the phone to the United States'.[65]

Blair's relationship with Bush, consummated during this period, is key to an understanding of his policy in the 'war on terror', and the degree to which it has been shaped by considerations of personality and power is an important issue which merits separate attention.

Relationship with George Bush and neoconservatives in the administration

An enduring puzzle has surrounded the Tony Blair/George W. Bush era: why did two politicians with very different backgrounds and who are from opposite ends of the ideological spectrum seem to be so compatible in foreign policy and interpersonal terms? Indeed, while the close Clinton/Blair relationship made some sense from an ideological standpoint, there was a good degree of trepidation on the British side as to whether President Bush and the prime minister would work effectively together.

As noted earlier, realist considerations of power created for Blair very strong incentives to ensure a positive relationship with Bush. Individual-level factors do also seem to have reinforced the realpolitik imperatives. Like Blair, Bush saw international affairs predominantly in black-and-white terms. Both were comfortable with 'the language of judgment and the politics of the simple assertion'.[66] The issue of international terrorism and rogue states provided a shared set of issues they saw as amenable to clear-cut, uncomplicated analysis: 'There were no shades of grey here: Osama bin Laden, Saddam Hussein and his fellow travellers were evil people.'[67] Sir Christopher Meyer, UK ambassador to the US, comments that 'I do think Blair and Bush were very taken by the notion that there was evil stalking the globe',[68] and David Blunkett agrees that Bush and Blair, for all the areas in which they were different, shared beliefs 'about doing the right thing and doing good, and not tolerating evil'.[69] Some have suggested that it was a shared Christian belief that is at the heart of this worldview, but it is worth noting that Blair, while genuinely religious, disliked the fundamentalist right wing in the United States and did not share their politics. Rather than religiosity per se defining a compatibility of worldview, shared lower conceptual complexity made both leaders comfortable with black-and-white judgments about the international environment.

A further area of compatibility sometimes suggested is the ambitious agenda of some of Bush's neo-conservative advisers and Blair's proactive international stance rooted in his high belief in his ability to control events. Neoconservatives believe in the effectiveness of bold international actions, particularly the ability of the United States to promote regime change in a democratic direction through the direct application of hard power. This does raise the significant question of whether Blair's foreign policy made him, in effect, a neoconservative. Elements of his 'Doctrine of International Community' analysed in Chapter 4, in particular the suggestion that the traditional restrictions on intervention in sovereign nations be loosened, could fit within a neoconservative worldview. Indeed, Blair's Chicago speech elucidating this doctrine was reprinted approvingly in a prominent collection of neoconservative writings.[71] There are certainly areas of overlap, as Dumbrell points out, between 'Blair's 'post-Westphalian' international liberalism and the Bush administration's post-9/11 commitment to democracy promotion'.[72] However, the overlap is not total. Dumbrell sees Blair as essentially a 'Third Way Clinton liberal' in foreign affairs, although, as seen in the Kosovo episode, he was often more hawkish than President Clinton.

While Blair's muscular liberalism and the Bush administration's neoconservatism did overlap in the post 9/11 period, they did also begin from different premises. Neoconservatism is more directly concerned with hard power, national security, and the need to identify and do battle with enemies, while Blair combined a strong security narrative with a focus on justice, morality, and human rights.[73] James Naughtie, noting Blair's lack of travel in the US, narrow circle of American friends, and failure to read deeply into modern American political history, not only doubts that Blair was a neoconservative but also raises compelling questions as to whether he fully understood either the provenance or the principles of the movement.[74] Clare Short is of the view that he never read the key public documents and position papers of the foreign policy neoconservatives.[74] Blunkett judges that Blair, while not sharing the neoconservative belief in 'messianic change' brought about solely by US power, did have 'the same kind of direction and certainty ... what he wants to do is to establish functioning democracies and to believe that politics is a way of resolving the world's major evils'.[76]

Blair himself commented that:

> I never really understand what people mean by this neocon thing. I come at this from a completely different perspective – a progressive perspective that says there not be a doctrine of non-intervention in every set of circumstances. Why should the left never support that? Why should we say that we should never intervene in a situation where people are brutally repressive? I mean I can't understand why we should be saying that. I can understand a right-wing conservative saying that. Now, I think after 9/11 from the other perspective there are people on the Right who have said – and I think this is where the progressive and right-wing cases come together – not 'we've got to go out and impose American values'. What I think people are saying, and this is certainly my belief, is that the greater the spread of freedom and democracy, the greater the possibility of security. Why? Because it is states that are repressed, that are dictatorial, that give their people no freedom, that don't allow them to exercise democratic rights that in my experience and judgment are the states that end up threatening others.[77]

This is certainly part of neoconservatism, and an area of congruence with Blair's own interventionist beliefs. However, the belief that democracy is generally a good idea is not the entirety of the neocon belief system, and there are legitimate questions, raised more than answered by the quotation above, as to whether Blair accurately read or understood the other impulses of this group.

These principles are not hard to locate: the views of those neoconservatives within the Bush administration were clearly expressed in a document Paul Wolfowitz, then under secretary of defense for policy in Dick Cheney's Pentagon, produced as far back as 1992, and that was immediately leaked to the *New York Times*. Preparation of the document involved not only Cheney and Wolfowitz, but also I. Lewis 'Scooter' Libby and Zalmay Khalilzad.[78] This document was expanded upon by the Project for the New American Century report in 2000, and neoconservatives in and out of government have written widely on their principles in prominent newspapers and journals. A distillation of these ideas into a heavily publicized 'Statement of Principles' was signed in 1997 by many who would subsequently occupy positions in the Bush administration: Elliott Abrams, Dick Cheney, Khalilzad, Libby, Donald Rumsfeld, and Wolfowitz.[79] This is to say that it is a relatively straightforward matter to reconstruct the foreign policy principles of neoconservatism from the public record, and that Blair's apparent failure to understand the beliefs of those to whom he was becoming committed is not due to their being particularly chaste in opining them.

1 To maintain unrivalled US military power

Wolfowitz had written in the 1992 Defense Planning Guide (DPG) that the US should not only maintain a pre-eminent position, but should be so powerful as to discourage even the attempt by others to compete. America must, he argued, 'maintain the mechanisms for deterring potential competitors from even aspiring to a larger regional or global role'.[80] He believed that the unipolar system which had emerged following the collapse of the Soviet Union need not be temporary, as many had assumed it would inevitably be, but could be preserved indefinitely if the United States had the will to commit sufficient resources. Neoconservatives suggested that there was little downside to maintaining primacy. To the argument that an America that maintains massive military forces would provoke rather than deter competitors, neoconservatives suggested that whatever the US did, it would be resented, so it may as well act aggressively to protect its interests and promote its values.[81] Besides which, the efforts of others, such as France, Russia, and China, to create a more balanced international system were ultimately posturing – none of these countries were willing to pay the price necessary to genuinely compete with the United States, so long as the hegemon did not succumb to sloth and irresolution. To accomplish the maintenance of primacy, defence spending increases above the level of the Clinton years were necessary and desirable, as was a general willingness of US leaders to face the 'true cost of security'.[82] 'If an American peace is to be maintained', the seminal neoconservative report on Rebuilding America's Defenses proclaimed, 'it must have a secure foundation on unquestioned US military preeminence'.[83]

2 The doctrines of pre-emption and regime change

The legitimacy of a pre-emptive policy and a doctrine of regime change came, in the neoconservative belief system, from the changed nature of security threats after the cold war. Traditional deterrence, they averred, could not work against rogue states and transnational terrorist groups. Deterrence relies upon the rationality of the opponent and the certainty of retaliatory action against any aggressive move. When these two conditions hold, opponents will anticipate the certainty of devastating retaliation, and so, being rational, will not act so as to provoke it. There is, however, no guarantee of rationality in the leadership of rogue states, neoconservatives suggested. Rogue regimes, rather than taking the disparity in power between themselves and the United States as motivation to be inoffensive, instead go 'looking for an equalizing advantage', most easily accomplished by their seeking 'to acquire their own weapons of mass destruction'.

Given this, nonproliferation agreements and traditional deterrent postures could not be relied upon, because many of the regimes seeking weapons could be trusted neither to adhere to agreements nor accurately to calculate the costs of their course of action. As Kristol and Kagan elaborate: 'The most effective form of non-proliferation when it comes to regimes such as those in North Korea and Iraq is not a continuing effort to bribe them into adhering to international arms control agreements, but an effort to bring about the demise of the regimes themselves.'[85]

The same broad-brush approach was to be adopted in regard to international terrorism after 9/11. International terrorists were not only non-rational, but had no defined territory or assets that could be attacked in retaliation. Therefore, international terrorism could be dealt with only by focusing upon regimes that support it: 'We make no distinction', stated the September 2002 National Security Strategy, 'between terrorists and those who knowingly harbor or provide aid to them'.[86] The non-visible nature of international terrorism, the lack of applicability of 'traditional concepts of deterrence', and the 'overlap between states that sponsor terror and those that pursue WMD'[87] legitimized for the neoconservatives a pre-emptive posture that sought to eliminate threats before they fully materialized and before, by definition, incontrovertible proof of their potency and imminence was available.

3 Democracy is a universal concept that can be spread through the application of hard power

People everywhere, for neoconservatives, want to choose their rulers and experience personal freedom. These are not desires specific to the Western world. Therefore, the creation of democracies is simply a matter of 'knocking off the head' of undemocratic regions, and allowing the populace's innate democratic urges to come into play. A democratic government would then organically emerge without much trouble. As the September 2002 National Security Strategy proclaimed, 'People everywhere want to be able to speak freely; choose who will govern them; worship as they please'. These universal impulses could be unleashed by the US shaping, in the slightly curious phase apparently crafted by Condeleeza Rice, 'a balance of power that favors human freedom'.[88]

4 Disdain or distrust for international institutions and multilateralism

Again, this was part of the DPG document from 1992, which was 'conspicuously devoid of references to collective action through the United Nations',[89] an especially noteworthy omission in the aftermath of the first Gulf war, one of the more spectacularly successful multilateral ventures of the latter twentieth century. Instead, the document suggested the US should 'be postured to act independently when collective action cannot be orchestrated'.[90]

For neoconservatives, there was in fact little good that could come out of international institutions, but there were many dangers. The United States, acting on behalf of universal values and pure motives, did not require the endorsement of other states to legitimize its actions. As the hegemonic power, few countries could meaningfully contribute to US military strength, and so the practical benefits were also marginal. But if the benefits of international institutions were unclear, the dangers were stark. Being unable to impose their will upon the US by force, other states would seek to restrain American freedom of action by ensnaring the US in a web of treaties, agreements, rules, and negotiations. Rogue states and terrorist groups could thus escape their fate if the United States waited for the approval of irresolute and bureaucratic international institutions – approval which was necessary neither practically nor morally.

A similar analysis prompted neoconservatives to be wary of conceding much in order to create and maintain multilateral coalitions. Wolfowitz had written in the DPG that 'we should expect future coalitions to be ad hoc assemblies, often not lasting beyond the crisis being confronted, and in many cases carrying only general agreement over the objectives to be accomplished'.[91] These coalitions would come together not by the US being consultative and deliberative, but by America giving strong and decisive leadership. Wolfowitz expanded upon these ideas in the late 1990s, arguing that America's European allies in particular were by nature followers, and would fall into line if the US gave a decisive lead: 'A willingness to act unilaterally can be the most effective way of securing effective collective action'.[92] Besides, allies were viewed not as force multipliers, but as troublesome free-riders who would merely constrain US freedom of action with their expectations of consultation and a share in decision making.[93]

5 The importance of Israel

This is a more controversial inclusion. Neoconservatives have complained that, due to several of their number being Jewish, they were accused of putting Israeli interests before those of America, and of being a shadowy and conspiratorial group of the like that has tended to pop up in anti-Semitic propaganda. Nonetheless, the views of neoconservatives on Israel are significant to our analysis, given the importance Blair placed on the Israel-Palestine conflict and the effort he expended to try to get the Bush administration involved in a sustained and balanced fashion.

Two things seem significant. First, as the only democracy in the region, and a state under regular attack from terrorist groupings, neoconservative ideology was extremely favourable toward Israel. In particular, given the neoconservative belief in the efficacy of force in effecting change and the irrelevance of international processes, the demonstration of strength and the taking of unilateral actions by Israeli governments was seen as perfectly legitimate from a neoconservative standpoint. The second relevant consideration is that several American neoconservatives, including 'Scooter' Libby, consulted with the Likud party of (at the time) Ariel Sharon, and helped draft its hawkish policy platform.

Much of the above stands outside of Blair's belief system, particularly the disdain for multilateral institutions and coalition building, and the strong 'tilt' toward Israel in the Middle East peace process. That Blair, as I contend, did not accurately grasp the entirety of this package of beliefs is not inexplicable: neoconservatism is, as George Packer explains, the product of a strange mix of influences: 'A European-produced, deliberately elitist, twilit view of the modern world was somehow wedded to the sunny all-American politics of triumphal capitalism, cultural piety, and flag-waving nationalism, under the most anti-intellectual president since at least Warren G. Harding.'[94] Blair had little in his background that would sensitize him to these influences: he did not read Strauss, had not lived or travelled widely in the United States, and had formative foreign policy experiences very different from those of the neoconservatives. Those around Bush had been out of office during the 1990s, and so had not engaged in the post-cold war debates about humanitarian war and the challenges of nation-building – exemplified by Kosovo and Sierra Leone, which were Blair's initial ventures into international affairs.

Instead, the neoconservatives' dominant foreign policy experience was Ronald Reagan's boldness and unapologetic promotion of American values as inherently good, his bellicose rhetoric and massive defence spending, and the perceived lesson that this had frightened the Soviet Union into defeat and led to bloodless democratic revolutions across Eastern Europe. Many of those around the president therefore started from a very different place than Tony Blair, and there is little evidence, crucially, that the prime minister realized the implications of this. Not everyone in the Bush administration was a neoconservative, nor were all their ideas applied with perfect fidelity. But, as Kristol puts it, after 9/11 'suddenly there was a lot more receptivity to the argument that the world was more dangerous than it seemed in the 1990s. Suddenly ... the case for regime change and democracy promotion as goals of American foreign policy seemed more compelling.'[95]

As we will see in the following chapter, however, the implications of Blair's ignorance of neoconservatism were profound: why, otherwise, would he have made his two (non-binding) conditions for support of the Iraq war that it be done through the United Nations and be accompanied by a solution to the Israel-Palestine conflict? Looking back from 2007, the former member of the cabinet Chris Smith noted that if, as many suspect, Blair did not understand what neoconservatism was in 2002, 'he probably does now'.[96]

What difference did Blair make?

Does analysis of Blair as an individual add importantly to our understanding of the close relationship he formed with the George Bush administration during this period? Again, the issues of *actor* and *action* dispensability are paramount. Would any person in the post of British prime minister have acted as Blair did in response to 9/11? What difference did Blair's actions make to American policy and to events more generally?.

Blair's response of genuine alarm and sympathy, and his offers of assistance following 9/11, was not markedly different from that of other world leaders, and so we do not need to look to his individual characteristics to explain his actions in the immediate aftermath of the attacks. His perception of the proper shape of the response, and the breadth and scope entailed, do require a closer look at Blair as an individual. As noted, there is a convincing argument that the war on Afghanistan is explicable in basic realist terms: the harbouring of Al Qaeda by the Taliban posed a continued threat, and removal of that threat was justified following an indisputable demonstration of its potency.

What was more distinctly Blairite, however, was the wider agenda he set out, and the desire not only to remove the specific danger of Al Qaeda, but to create a new international order where such threats would simply not exist. This involved .

> an unequivocal commitment to defeating Al Qaeda and other similar terrorists, initially in Afghanistan and then beyond; doing so multinationally by building an international coalition of support; the search for a breakthrough in the Middle East peace process, and winning over world opinion.[97]

Charles Powell, former foreign policy adviser to Margaret Thatcher, judges that Blair supported 'an adjustment of foreign policy to give priority for dealing with the problems of terrorism, of terrorist states, of dictators with weapons of mass destruction. I think that was the right decision to make, but not every prime minister would have made it.'[98]

Indeed, this agenda contained some very distinctly Blairite elements in its ambition, the importance of preserving the moral high ground in the eyes of world opinion, and the focus on root-cause problems. As Mathew D'Ancona explains 'it's not simply about defence. It's not simply about targeting your enemies and destroying them. It's actually about creating an entirely new global environment, in which phenomena like Al Qaeda, rogue states like Iraq, simply don't happen.'[99] While British support for the United States following the attacks and endorsement of war with Afghanistan was likely with anyone as prime minister given the strategic considerations involved, the shape and scope of that support can plausibly be related quite directly to Blair himself.

The subsequent question is then one of *action dispensability*: did Blair materially affect the course of events during this period? If he had not been prime minister, what would have been different?.

Blair's first goal post 9/11 was to ensure that the United States' response would be judicious and measured. There was a fear that the president, without much foreign affairs experience and leading a nation in deep shock, might quickly take ill-considered actions that would do little more than inflame Middle East opinion and squander America's moral capital. On 12 September, Blair had told Bush that the choice was between 'rapid action and effective action'. In particular, an immediate attack on Iraq, which the British had learned was being advocated by some in the Bush administration, would be unwise. As Christopher Meyer explained, 'Tony Blair's view was that whatever you're going to do about Iraq, you should concentrate on the job at hand, and the job at hand was to get Al Qaeda. Give the Taliban an ultimatum, and everything else was secondary to that.'[100] This was of course what happened, and on Blair's November visit the president took Blair aside and told him 'I agree with you, Tony. Afghanistan is the priority. We will come back to Iraq in due course.'[101]

However, there is some evidence that while Blair's preferences correlate with the policy outcome in this instance, a causal relationship is more difficult to establish. Others within the administration, in particular Colin Powell and the State Department, had reached the same conclusion, and indeed in the weekend following the 9/11 attacks had won an internal administration argument over whether to focus narrowly on Afghanistan or also attack Iraq.[102] Powell had told the president that going after Iraq would fracture the incipient coalition internationally and be risky domestically.[103] Blair's intervention was therefore 'not crucial. He did not change US policy'.[104] As Con Coughlin speculates, 'had Bush's war cabinet been more determined at Camp David to press for an immediate attack against Iraq, Blair would have been placed in a very difficult position'.[105] However, fortunately for the prime minister 'Bush had independently reached the same conclusions as Blair'. Unfortunately for Blair, this would be the last argument of any significance Colin Powell won within the administration.

Blair did not succeed, however, in decisively convincing Bush that working with allies was the most effective way to deal with the ramifications of 9/11. Pondering Blair's entreaties as to the value of multilateralism, Bush was cautious. 'At some point', the president told Colin Powell, 'we may be the only ones left. That's okay with me. We are America.'[106] Woodward includes a later account of Bush reporting a conversation with a 'European leader' (there is no indication as to whether this was Blair or not, but it does sound like him):

> who said the way to maintain the coalition was to have lots of consultation, for the U.S. to show responsiveness, take account of the views of others and understand their reasoning. 'Well', he said, 'that's very interesting. Because my belief is the best way that we hold this coalition together is to be clear on our objectives and to be clear that we are determined to achieve them. You hold a coalition together by strong leadership and that's what we intend to provide.[107]

This statement, which shows Bush moving increasingly toward a unilateralist worldview following 9/11, would portend great difficulty for Blair in the future.

His second major effort was made on the question of the Israel-Palestine dispute. Blair believed that resolution of this dispute, and in particular the application of pressure upon the hard-line Ariel Sharon government to make concessions and publishing the so-called 'road map to peace' with the full endorsement of the United States, would be a hugely progressive step in depriving terrorist groups of wider support and securing the moral high ground. As Seldon puts it:

> It was Blair's great hope to show that, out of the horror of 9/11, a more just world would result, with the principal cause of Muslin hostility to the West, the denial of a sustainable state for Palestinians, lanced ... Only with the Americans on board, he reasoned, would there be any hope of persuading Ariel Sharon and his Likud party to make the necessary concessions.[108]

Sir Christopher Meyer, ambassador to the United States, calls this a 'very, very big factor' in what Blair was saying to the United States,[109] and sees it as central to avoiding the appearance of a 'war of civilizations between Muslins and Christians'.[110] John Sawers, a senior diplomat, notes that Blair approached this in very personal terms: 'He always saw Israel/Palestine through the prism of Northern Ireland. He had a belief in his own powers of persuasion and bringing people together to achieve a common end.'[111]

In November of 2001, Blair pressed Bush directly on this matter, telling him that the Arab-Israeli conflict was central to the war on terror, and that failing to move on the peace process 'risks alienating Arab opinion'.[112] However, although the Bush administration did eventually publish the 'roadmap' in January 2003, little pressure was applied upon the Sharon government to implement it.[113] The Foreign Office, in fact, viewed Blair's efforts as largely futile, with a senior official commenting that 'Hell is likely to freeze over before Bush is ready to treat Sharon with a big stick'.[114] Sharon himself made doubly sure that Blair would not succeed by warning the US 'do not try to appease the Arabs at our expense. Israel will not be Czechoslovakia.'[115] Indeed, the president resisted Blair's attempt to link progress on Israel-Palestine to success in the 'war on terror', stating that 'we will bring Al Qaeda to justice, peace or no peace in the Middle East'.[116] Meyer summed up Blair's lack of impact on Bush's Palestine policy a little more diplomatically: 'on the whole, that was not an argument where we made as much progress as we would have wished to have made.'[117] A senior White House aide suggests that 'our views on Israel were just poles apart from Blair's. Blair just didn't understand our concerns. We felt Blair was hopelessly optimistic on the Middle East, and far too respectful of Arafat, whom we regarded as the embodiment of the problem. For that reason, it [Blair's efforts] had no influence or impact here.'[118] Ken Adelman was even more blunt:

> I always thought that Blair's pleas for progress on the Middle East were a lot of BS. It was nice listening to him talking about it. It was the kind of stuff you'd expect from a European leader. So you kept on saying 'Yeah, OK, OK, we have all the intention in the world', but the fact is the players weren't there, the timing wasn't there, the substance wasn't there. Tony Blair would respond, 'Yes, but you have to create all those'. It just wasn't going to happen.[119]

Blair was not the only one pushing this point with little success – his policy agenda and influence was in fact increasingly tied to the fortunes of secretary of state Colin Powell. During this period, Powell was dispatched to the Middle East but told to only meet Sharon and not Arafat, and to soft-peddle the peace process with the Israeli leader. Powell's frustrations at being sent on an effectively impossible mission – to make peace by talking with only one side to the conflict – were significant: 'No one [in the administration] wanted to face reality!' he is reported as saying. 'They wanted to be pro-Israel and leave him holding the Palestinian bag by himself.'[120]

An indicator of Powell's concern over his declining influence in relation to Cheney, Rumsfeld and Wolfowitz is that on returning from this trip he requested regular one-on-one time with the president and redoubled his efforts to forge a close personal relationship with Bush, with whom he had little natural chemistry.[121] This was a dangerous situation for Blair, who had been reassured by the alignment of preferences between himself and the US secretary of state but was, it seemed, backing a losing horse. It would become increasingly obvious that Cheney and Rumsfeld were far more effective at winning intra-administration battles than Powell and, given that neither had much time for Blair or his policy views, this began to pose a serious problem for the British prime minister.

In the period following the September 11 attacks, then, Blair had consolidated his position as the number one ally of the United States and generated great political capital with the American public and some in the administration. He had outlined an ambitious new application of his foreign policy style, focused upon the nexus of rogue states, terrorist groups, and weapons of mass destruction. He had kept on the agenda the issue he saw as fundamental to a comprehensive Middle East policy – resolution of the Israeli-Palestinian conflict. This was all to the good. However, Blair had failed in generating support in the Middle East for the Afghanistan war, and in securing a decisive commitment to the peace process, with genuine pressure upon Sharon, from Bush. Dynamics within the US administration had during this period tilted bureaucratically in favour of Cheney and Rumsfeld, and ideationally toward the neoconservatives, and there is little evidence that Blair recognized the significance of these developments. As the Afghanistan campaign concluded and the focus of the United States shifted increasingly to Iraq, some in the UK feared Blair, with his staunch support for President Bush, might have tipped his hand too soon.

Blair himself said at the time:

In the end, Britain is a sovereign nation. Britain decides its own policy and although I back America I would never back America if I thought they were doing something wrong. I wouldn't support it. But I've never found that, and I don't expect to find it in the future.[122]

Privately, Blair's judgment – one I find difficult to sustain on examination of the evidence – was that he was exercising considerable influence over Bush's policies: 'Bluntly', he told a friend in March of 2002, 'I am the one Western leader the U.S. will really listen to.'[123] Blair would perhaps have been interested to know of a happening in the White House at about the same time. President Bush, wandering the halls, poked his head around a door and interrupted a meeting on Iraq policy between the national security adviser Condeleeza Rice and several US senators: 'Fuck Saddam', Bush said. 'We're taking him out.'[124]

Notes

1 C. Coughlin, *American Ally* (New York: HarperCollins, 2006), p. 113.
2 Ibid., p. 152.
3 P. Sands, *Lawless World: America and the Making and Breaking of Global Rules from FDR's Atlantic Charter to George W. Bush's Illegal War* (New York: Viking, 2005), p. 174.
4 Quoted in T. Ricks, *Fiasco: The American Military Adventure in Iraq* (New York: Penguin, 2006), p. 30.
5 Ibid., p. 31.
6 Coughlin, *American Ally*, p. 154; see also A. Danchev, 'I'm with you: Tony Blair and the obligations of alliances: Anglo American relations in historical perspective', in L. C. Gardner and M. B. Young (eds), *Iraq and the Lessons of Vietnam* (New York: The New Press, 2007), p. 49.
7 P. Riddell, *The Unfulfilled Prime Minister: Tony Blair's Quest for a Legacy* (London: Politico's, 2006), p. 139.
8 D. Blunkett, *The Blunkett Tapes: My Life in the Bear Pit* (London: Bloomsbury, 2006), p. 292.
9 A. Seldon, *Blair* (London: Free Press, 2004), p. 618.
10 B. Woodward, *Bush at War* (New York: Simon & Schuster, 2002), p. 44.
11 Ricks, *Fiasco*, p. 31.
12 Woodward, *Bush at War*, p. 63.
13 P. Riddell, *Hug Them Close: Blair, Clinton, Bush and the 'Special Relationship'* (London: Politico's, 2003), pp. 156–7.
14 S. Azubuike, 'Still buying insurance? The realism behind Tony Blair's post-September 11th evangelization', *The Review of International Affairs*, 3:1 (2003), 70.
15 Riddell, *The Unfulfilled Prime Minister*, p. 140.
16 Coughlin, *American Ally*, p. 174.
17 Blunkett, *My Life in the Bear Pit*.

18 A. Seldon, *Blair Unbound* (New York: Simon & Schuster, 2007).

19 Coughlin, *American Ally*, p. 172.

20 J. Mann, *Rise of the Vulcans: The History of Bush's War Cabinet* (New York: Penguin, 2004), p. 304.

21 P. Stephens, *Tony Blair: The Making of a World Leader* (New York: Viking, 2004), p. 194.

22 Ibid., p. 198.

23 J. Naughtie, *The Accidental American: Tony Blair and the Presidency* (New York: Public Affairs, 2004), p. 17.

24 Coughlin, *American Ally*, p. 144.

25 Author interview with Sir Jeremy Greenstock, 6 June 2007.

26 Author interview with David Blunkett, 1 May 2007.

27 Danchev, 'I'm with you', p. 50.

28 Azubuike, 'Still buying insurance?', p. 74.

29 Coughlin, *American Ally*, p. 205.

30 Azubuike, 'Still buying insurance?', p. 72.

31 Tony Blair's Speech to the Labour Party Conference, Monday 1 October 2001. Available at http://politics.guardian.co.uk/print/o,,4268838-108975,00.html, accessed 3 October 2006.

32 *Frontline*, interview with Matthew D'Ancona, 11 March 2003. Available www.pbs.org/wgbh/pages/frontline/shows/blair/interviews/dancona.html, accessed 3 July 2007.

33 Naughtie, The Accidental American, p. 63.

34 Riddell, *Hug Them Close*, p. 166.

35 C. Short, *New Labour: An Honourable Deception?* (London: Simon & Schuster, 2004), p. 107.

36 Quoted in Riddell, *Hug Them Close*, p. 166.

37 E. MacAskill and M. White, 'Bold Blair takes the zealous road to war', *The Guardian*, 29 September 2001: 7.

38 Blunkett, *My Life in the Bear Pit*, p. 310.

39 Seldon, *Blair Unbound*, p. 62.

40 Seldon, *Blair*, p. 505.

41 Stephens, *Tony Blair*, p. 206.

42 Author interview with Clare Short, 30 April 2007.

43 Seldon, *Blair*, p. 484.

44 *Frontline*, interview with Tony Blair, 8 May 2002. Available at www.pbs.org/wgbh/pages/frontline/shows/campaign/interviews/blair.html, accessed 5 July 2007.

45 Seldon, *Blair*, p. 488.

46 P. Wintour, 'This is war, and we must act, says PM', *The Guardian*, Monday 17 September 2001.

47 Stephens, *Tony Blair*, p. 201.

48 Naughtie, *The Accidental American*, p. 21.

49 Tony Blair interviewed on BBC Radio 4, *The Today Programme*, Thursday 22 February 2007. Available at www.bbc.co.uk/radio4/today, retrieved 23 February 2007.

50 Short, *An Honourable Deception?*, p. 109.

51 Seldon, *Blair*, p. 497.

52 *Frontline*, interview with Charles Powell. Available at www.pbs.org/ wgbh/pages/frontline/shows/blair/prime/blairbush.html, accessed 5 July 2007.

53 Naughtie, *The Accidental American*, p. 58.

54 Ibid., p. 75.

55 *Frontline*, interview with Tony Blair.

56 Seldon, *Blair Unbound*, p. 57.

57 Naughtie, *The Accidental American*, p. 55.

58 P. Williams, *British Foreign Policy Under New Labour* (London: Palgrave Macmillan, 2005), p. 45.

59 Riddell, *Hug Them Close*, p. 146.

60 Seldon, *Blair*, p. 499.

61 MacAskill and White, 'Bold Blair takes the zealous road to war, p. 7.

62 A. Perkins, 'Blair: first among equals?', *The Guardian* 6 October 2001, p. 5.

63 Coughlin, *American Ally*, p. 210.

64 Naughtie, *The Accidental American*, p. 70; Stephens, *Tony Blair*, p. 112.

65 Author interview with Clare Short, 30 April 2007.

66 Naughtie, *The Accidental American*, pp. 58–9.

67 Seldon, *Blair*, p. 616.

68 G. Hinscliff, 'Blair's Christianity', *The Observer*, Sunday 8 April 2007. Available at http://politics.guardian.co.uk/labourleadership/story/ 0,,2053818,00.html, accessed 25 May 2007.

69 Author interview with David Blunkett, 1 May 2007.

70 Naughtie, *The Accidental American*, pp. 58–9.

71 I. Steltzer, *The Neocon Reader* (New York: Grove Press, 2004).

72 J. Dumbrell, 'Working with allies: the United States, the United Kingdom, and the war on terror', *Politics & Policy*, 34:2 (2006), p. 465.

73 Riddell, *Hug Them Close*, p. 170.

74 Naughtie, *The Accidental American*, pp. 89–90.

75 Author interview with Clare Short, 30 April 2007.

76 Author interview with David Blunkett, 1 May 2007.

77 Quoted in Naughtie, *The Accidental American*, p. 66-67.

78 Mann, *Rise of the Vulcans*, p. 210.

79 www.newamericancentury.org/statementofprinciples.htm, accessed 30 May 2007.

80 P. E. Tyler, 'US strategy plan calls for ensuring no rivals develop', *New York Times*, 8 March 1992, p. 1.

81 W. Kristol and R. Kagan, 'National interest and global responsibility', in Steltzer (ed.). *The Neocon Reader*, p. 72.

82 D. Kagan, G. Schmitt, and T. Donnelly, 'Rebuilding America's defenses': strategy, forces and resources for a new century', *A Report of The Project for the New American Century*, 2000: iii.

83 Ibid., p. 4.

84 Ibid., p. 7.

85 Kristol and Kagan, 'National interest and global responsibility', p. 69.

86 White House (2002), 'The National Security Strategy of the United States of America', September 2002. Available at www.whitehouse.gov/ nsc/nss.html, accessed 1 August 2007, p. 5.

87 Ibid, p. 15.
88 Ibid.
89 Tyler, 'US strategy plan'.
90 Ibid.
91 Ibid.
92 Mann, *Rise of the Vulcans*, p. 237.
93 Ibid., p. 362.
94 George Packer, *The Assassin's Gate* (New York: Farrar, Strauss and Giroux, 2005), p. 55.
95 William Kristol, 'Neoconservatism remains the bedrock of US foreign policy', in Stelzer (ed.), *The Neocon Reader*, pp. 75–6.
96 Author interview with Chris Smith, 18 June 2007.
97 Seldon, *Blair*, p. 493.
98 *Frontline*, interview with Charles Powell.
99 *Frontline*, interview with Matthew D'Ancona.
100 *Frontline*, interview with Sir Christopher Meyer, 18 March 2003. Available at www.pbs.org/wgbh/pages/frontline/shows/blair/interviews/meyer.html, accessed 5 June 2006.
101 Stephens, *Tony Blair*, p. 200.
102 Naughtie, *The Accidental American*, p. 60; Stephens, *Tony Blair*, p. 200.
103 Woodward, *Bush at War*, p. 84.
104 Riddell, *Hug Them Close*, p. 155.
104 Coughlin, *American Ally*, p. 168–9.
106 Woodward, *Bush at War*, p. 81.
107 Ibid, p. 281.
108 Seldon, *Blair*, p. 618.
109 *Frontline*, interview with Sir Christopher Meyer.
110 C. Meyer, *DC Confidential* (London: Weidenfeld and Nicholson, 2005), p. 191.
111 Seldon, *Blair Unbound*, p. 64.
112 E. MacAskill and R. N. Taylor, 'Splits open in UK-US alliance', *The Guardian*, 9 November 2001, p. 1.
113 Williams, *British Foreign Policy*, p. 194.
114 Seldon, *Blair*, p. 618.
115 Woodward, *Bush at War*, p. 197.
116 Quoted in Azubuike, 'Still buying insurance?', p. 77.
117 *Frontline*, interview with Sir Christopher Meyer.
118 Coughlin, *American Ally*, pp. 190; 229.
119 Seldon, *Blair Unbound*, p. 64.
120 Woodward, *Bush at War*, p. 324.
121 Woodward, *Bush at War*, p. 330.
122 Quoted in Naughtie, *The Accidental American*, p. 71.
123 Coughlin, *American Ally*, p. 210.
124 Packer, *The Assassin's Gate*, p. 45.

6 Iraq – Blair's war

The decision to invade Iraq is the most controversial of Blair's wars, undertaken without public support, and with significant disquiet among members of his government and political party. At several points it looked as though the decision to go to war could cost the prime minister his job – an incredible turn-around for a politician used to great popularity and colossal parliamentary majorities. Blair didn't waver. Once it became clear that the Bush administration was set on its course, strong incentives existed from an alliance maintenance standpoint to join them. Further, Blair, with his Manichean view of international politics, shared much of the analysis of the Bush administration about the threat of weapons of mass destruction, irrational dictators, and potential connections with terrorists. Blair's strong internal locus of control led him to downplay the risks in securing support for the war and in the war's ultimate success. Finally, his directive and hands-on decision style ensured that the significant opposition to the policy within his cabinet and foreign office was marginalized at the crucial decision points.

The Iraq choices

The possibility of war with Iraq had been raised, as we saw in the previous chapter, in the immediate aftermath of the 11 September 2001 attacks. Then, Blair had counselled Bush to concentrate on the Taliban and Afghanistan. This the administration did, although not without some internal disagreement and, as we have seen, a good amount of questioning as to whether the moment was ripe for dealing with Saddam Hussein. Blair was, then, forewarned that the issue of Iraq would reappear on the agenda.

It did not take long to do so. Iraq policy dominated the April 2002 summit between Blair and Bush at the president's Crawford, Texas ranch. Blair and his key foreign affairs adviser Sir David Manning were met by a president seemingly determined to go to war. This shaped the framing Blair had of events – if the Americans were definitely going to go ahead, a choice had to be made: do the British seek to act as a very public restraint on war as France and Germany would, or support the United States while seeking to build as big a coalition as possible for action, and ensure that action was taken in a reasonable way? For Blair, the choice was clear: 'We're not going to be with the other Europeans. Our policy on Iraq has always been different to them. We've always been with the Americans on this one.'[1]

While the decision itself was, for Blair, not difficult, the political problems it presented were. President Bush's 2002 State of the Union address, during which he famously labelled Iran, Iraq, and North Korea as an 'axis of evil', had caused significant disquiet among the European allies and in the United Kingdom. A survey of members of Blair's Labour Party in February had found 86% disagreeing with the 'axis of evil' characterization, and a similar majority believing that there was no evidence to justify a military attack on Iraq.[2] Polls showed that public opinion also ran strongly against the prospect of war.[3]

Blair's domestic strategy was to deny that any decisions on Iraq had been made, and utilize the time this gave him to work for United Nations resolutions authorizing a war. Explicit UN authorization, the same polling data showed, would take most of the heat out of both public and parliamentary opposition. Therefore, Blair cautioned throughout the summer of 2002 against 'getting ahead of ourselves' on the issue of Iraq: 'Action is not imminent. We are not at the point of decision yet.'[4] In cabinet, Blair began trying to move colleagues toward the position he had reached in his private meetings with Bush. The prime minister was able to gain support around the principle of the potential threat posed by Saddam Hussein, predicated on the information in a government dossier on Iraq Weapons of Mass Destruction published on 24 September.[5] He was left in no doubt, however, that dealing with Iraq was not seen as a priority by cabinet, and that the view of colleagues was that the issue could not be resolved separate from wider Middle East questions. Blair gave assurances that he would work through the United Nations and that Israel-Palestine could be dealt with 'in tandem' with the issue of Iraq.[6]

Not everyone was reassured. Those on the left of the Labour party resolved at this point to 'hold Tony Blair's ankles whilst he held on to

George Bush', Clare Short writes. 'At this stage, I was concerned but hopeful that the Labour Party would be able to keep Tony Blair on the straight and narrow.'[7] Blair promised cabinet there would be no rushing in, but, his ally David Blunkett wrote, 'we all fear that they will'.[8]

Blair returned to see Bush at Camp David on 7 September, and argued that the most efficacious way to carry out the policy was to seek as many allies as possible, and that this entailed a good faith effort to work through the United Nations. He found the president willing to make this effort, although it would be suggested that this had more to do with similar arguments made by secretary of state Colin Powell than with direct influence by Blair. Polling of the American public that showed a majority wanted to work through the UN was surely influential as well. Nonetheless, Blair's overall policy had some coherence and was showing some progress at this point. He could reconcile his promises to the president and to his domestic audience if UN support could be secured, and Bush had agreed to try.

The president addressed the UN Security Council a few days later. The reception was not entirely warm. The contentious nature of the debate within the administration, with the Cheney-Rumsfeld-Wolfowitz axis sceptical of the UN and willing to take action without its imprimatur, was by now well-known internationally. Members of the Security Council were wary of being used to rubber-stamp a decision that had effectively been made already, mirroring in this respect some of the worries of the British cabinet. The Security Council was determined to keep 'automaticity' – some condition that if breached by Iraq would trigger the use of force – from being included in any resolution.

The president himself unwittingly complicated the situation with a verbal slip. His speech to the Security Council had undergone many revisions, and an older draft – not including an explicit request for a resolution – had been loaded into the autocue machine. Fortunately, the president noticed the omission, and sought to ad-lib the material later in the speech. Less adroitly, he stated that the US and UK would seek the 'relevant resolutions' – plural – giving an opening to the type of drawn-out, 'soupy' process that occupied the nightmares of the Cheney wing of the administration. Indeed, the re-admittance of weapons inspectors, which would be the actionable part of any new resolution, would for Cheney be a dangerous development:

> [A] person would be right to question any suggestion that we should just get inspectors back into Iraq, and then our worries will be over. Saddam has perfected the game of cheat and retreat, and is very skilled at the art of denial and deception. A return of inspectors would provide no assurance whatsoever of his compliance with UN resolutions. On the contrary, there is a great danger that it would provide false comfort that Saddam was somehow 'back in the box'.[9]

Cheney's approach was that the UN was not to be worked with, but 'made the issue, challenged and criticized' for a supine attitude to enforcing its resolutions on Iraq.[10]

The president's speech spurred action on what would become UN resolution 1441, demanding that Iraq re-admit weapons inspectors and make a full declaration about its WMD activities. Resolution 1441 was passed unanimously by the Security Council on 8 November 2002, and the foreign secretary, Jack Straw, was so pleased with it that he took to reciting large chunks from memory.[11] David Blunkett saw it as 'a very substantial victory for Tony's tremendous diplomacy'.[12]

It was not quite so clear cut as that. Resolution 1441 became an Iraq policy Rorschach test. For Blair, it signified that 'Everyone now accepts that if there is a default [on its provisions] by Saddam, the international community must act to enforce its will. Failure to do so would mean, having stated our clear demand, that we lacked the will to enforce it.'[13] However, Blair's foreign secretary, Jack Straw, took a different view, arguing that the resolution merely ensured the return of weapons inspectors to Iraq, without a deadline for completion of their work, and that the prospect of military action had therefore receded significantly.[14] The French read the resolution as containing no 'trigger' for action, and as enshrining the principle that any further moves would have to be debated and voted upon by the Security Council. Finally, the more hawkish elements in the Bush administration argued that 1441, in combination with the ceasefire resolutions that ended the first Persian Gulf war, provided more than sufficient legal authority for military action. While the resolution had been voted on unanimously, then, everyone thought it meant something different.

1441 was the highpoint of Blair's strategy, which now quickly began to crumble. First, Saddam Hussein agreed to readmit UN inspectors and to pull together documentation on Iraq's weapons activities, underlining the dangers of making demands in the hope that they will be refused – you find yourself in a rather difficult position if they are in fact accepted. Saddam's cooperation denied the US-UK alliance their first chance of a clear *casus belli* under UN auspicious, though the hope remained that the UN inspectors would discover hidden WMD stockpiles.

Second, the cabinet and parliamentary Labour party became increasingly restless over the rhetoric emanating from Washington, which seemed to imply war was inevitable, and the growing realization that the prime minister had every intention of standing with the United States come what may. In Cincinnati in early October the rhetoric from the president reached its apogee in ways distinctly unhelpful to Blair's domestic position:.

> Saddam Hussein still has chemical and biological weapons, and is increasing his capabilities to make more. And he is moving ever closer to developing a nuclear weapon ... America must not ignore the threat gathering against us. Facing clear evidence of peril, we cannot wait for the final proof, the smoking gun that could come in the form of a mushroom cloud.[15]

In the ranks of Blair's parliamentary Labour party, draft bills were circulated behind closed doors insisting that Britain not be part of any military action without UN authorization, and enough MPs signed on to indicate to Blair that he might not carry a majority of his own party under present circumstances.

Within the cabinet, Robin Cook, the leader of the House of Commons and former foreign secretary, was asking increasingly pointed and well-chosen questions about the policy, while Clare Short, the international development secretary, was known to be unhappy and even contemplating resignation. Several others in the cabinet, including Blair allies, were very uneasy about the direction of events. The British public was unconvinced of the case for war and had not accepted 1441 as constituting UN approval for action. Internationally, President Chirac of France and Chancellor Schroeder of Germany had by now become heroes in their own countries by opposing the US-UK's Iraq policy, and had effectively joined Russia and China in open opposition to the Bush administration's aims.

As 2003 began, then, a senior cabinet colleague feared for the prime minister: 'Tony was making the classic political error. He has got himself into a situation with no exit strategy. He became subject to forces he could not control.'[16] David Blunkett was concerned enough to note in his diary that 'It is all getting very nasty now',[17] and Clare Short observed the personal toll the pressure was taking on Blair: 'his face became thin, and he looked gray. He was getting to the edge of the risk he'd taken.'[18] Indeed, Blair's options had narrowed severely, and he now realized he needed a second UN resolution, one that explicitly authorized military force. However, this was not in his gift – first, President Bush would have to agree to seek such a resolution, and second, the French and others on the Security Council would have to agree to grant it.

Blair travelled to try and persuade Bush at the end of January. This was a hard sell and, as David Manning's minutes of the meeting record, the president insisted that '[o]ur diplomatic strategy had to be arranged around the military planning'. All the talking, Bush said, had to be concluded by March, as 'this was when the bombing would begin'. Blair made clear how much he needed a second resolution for domestic political purposes, and sought to persuade Bush that it would serve as

> an insurance policy against the unexpected. If anything went wrong with the military campaign, or if Saddam increased the stakes by burning the oil wells, killing children, or fomenting internal divisions within Iraq, a second resolution would give us international cover, especially with the Arabs.

Bush agreed to seek such a resolution, but concluded discussions by stating that 'if we ultimately failed [to obtain UN support], military action would follow anyway'.[19]

Efforts by the British and the Americans to make the case that Saddam was a major threat were redoubled. In early February Colin Powell made a presentation to the UN Security Council, making public many of the juicy tidbits of intelligence the administration had shovelled together. Powell made creative use of props, including vials of a curious looking liquid that he waved above his head and colourful diagrams of suspicious trucks and laboratories. Powell was a convincing advocate, and his great prestige ensured a respectful reception, although the impression remained that the briefing was more style than substance.

In the UK, the intelligence case made by the government did not fare even this well. A dossier on Iraq's weapons was released, with a personal foreword from Blair. This contained the eye-catching claim that Iraq had weapons of mass destruction that could be launched – the implication was against British targets – within forty-five minutes of an order being given. The revelation made front-page news, but did not withstand expert analysis. Worse was that much of the body of the dossier, marketed as the best the UK intelligence services had gathered, was quickly exposed as inexpertly plagiarized from an old PhD thesis.

The affair of the so-called 'dodgy dossier' did much to undermine the credibility of Blair's assertions on the Iraqi threat and confirm the public in their scepticism. Jack Straw had little knowledge of the dossier beforehand and reportedly 'went ballistic' on hearing of it[20] while Robin Cook, who was becoming increasingly baffled by Blair's actions, called it 'a glorious, spectacular own goal'.[21]

The push for a second United Nations resolution, one that explicitly authorized the use of force against Iraq, had thus begun inauspiciously, with the efforts to prove Saddam's possession of WMD being unconvincing if not slightly farcical. The situation was not helped by the first of chief weapons inspector Hans Blix's reports to the Security Council on 14 February. Blix reported substantial Iraqi cooperation, and a failure so far to locate any suspicious weapons. Domestic opposition to the war in the UK now spilled over into public protest. The next day over a million people took to the streets of London for a 'Stop the War' rally. It was the largest public demonstration in British history.

As March began, Blair's prospects for rescuing the situation rested entirely on happenings in the UN. The French were threatening to veto the second resolution, but Blair's judgment was that if a majority of the fifteen members of the Security Council could be secured, then the French would be under great pressure to abstain and the measure would pass. Robin Cook reports that in the House and during cabinet meetings at this time, Blair was 'surprisingly upbeat' about getting the majority. Cook could not tell 'whether this is calculated bravado to keep Saddam wary, or whether he is in a state of denial about the mounting evidence that they can't get a second resolution on the present terms'. Either way, in Cook's judgment, Blair's plan of gaining a majority and then compelling the French to abstain was 'not just surprising but manifestly unrealistic'.[22] And Cook was by now far from the only cabinet minister uncomfortable with the way policy was headed.

The foreign secretary, Jack Straw, receiving dire analyses from the Foreign Office about the likely postwar situation in Iraq, composed a memo to Blair suggesting that if a second resolution could not be obtained and public support not secured, UK troops should not join in combat operations but could instead enter Iraq later in a peacekeeping role.[23] Indeed, President Bush himself, fearing that Blair's government might actually fall over the issue, offered the same solution. 'If they don't vote with us', Bush said to Blair, 'what I want to say to you is that my last choice is to have your government go down. We don't want to have that happen in any circumstances.' Echoing

Straw, Bush said British troops could join as 'a second wave, peace-keepers or something. I would rather go alone than have your government fall'. Indeed, the evidence is that the United States was reasonably sanguine about the question of ultimate British participation, with the secretary of defense, Donald Rumsfeld, stating bluntly that the troops were basically inessential to the operation.[24] Blair would not consider staying out, and said in reply to Bush's offer: 'I said I'm with you, I mean it … I absolutely believe in this too … I'm there to the very end.'[25]

However, the UN side of things was proving intractable. Blair, frantic to secure a resolution, was lobbying at a fearsome pace for the votes of uncommitted countries. He suggested to Clare Short that he might visit Chile, a non-permanent member of the council, to ask personally for their vote. 'I don't think there's much point', she counselled him, 'you're just humiliating yourself'.[26] Blair by now faced an almost impossible task in securing Security Council support, says Britain's then ambassador to the United Nations, Sir Jeremy Greenstock. Several members of the Security Council had the perception that

> the Americans weren't listening to anybody else, the Americans were going to do what they were going to do and they weren't very interested in the UN episode from September onwards. They wouldn't really listen to or understand the need to try and stop the international community from falling apart.[27]

This perception had become especially lodged in the mindset of the French who, Greenstock confirms, had ceased to judge the issue in terms of Iraq and Saddam Hussein and were instead concentrating on 'their antagonism to America acting unilaterally'.[28] In the midst of the frantic British lobbying of the Security Council, French President Chirac delivered the coup de grace. Drawing himself up to his maximum grandiosity, he proclaimed on national television on 10 March that war was unjustified, and France would veto any resolution authorizing it. 'My position', announced Chirac, 'is that, regardless of the circumstances, France will vote no because it considers this evening there are no grounds for waging war in order to achieve the goal we have set ourselves – to disarm Iraq'.[29] This rendered Blair's diplomatic efforts moot, and ensured that the war would occur without UN backing.

Blair's political position was now incredibly tenuous, and his survival in office in grave doubt. The one silver lining was that Chirac's speech had contained a whiff of grandiloquence, just enough for Blair to put it about that the French veto was unreasonable, and UN backing would have been forthcoming without it. This was a tenuous case at best, which the European commissioner Chris Pattern would later call 'pathetic',[30] but it took just enough attention away from the failure to secure UN support as to keep Blair alive politically.

With the international effort having crashed in spectacular fashion, could Blair hold the line domestically? Matters now came to a head. Having been slow handclapped by members of the public in a televised 'town hall' style meeting, Blair returned to Downing Street to try to draw together his cabinet and win a parliamentary vote authorizing British participation in the war. At a private dinner on 11 March, Blair was able to shore up support from his deputy, John Prescott, and the powerful chancellor of the exchequer, Gordon Brown.[31] Rumours had circulated that Brown was quite enjoying the discomfort of the prime minister and strongly suspected Blair might not survive, leaving the chancellor in pole position to take over. Indeed, David Blunkett indicates that while 'I never heard Gordon resile from the decisions that were being taken … it was rather late in the day when he joined in publicly'.[32]

Matters did not improve for Blair when he was confronted the same night by a radio interview given by Clare Short denouncing his Iraq policy as 'reckless with the government, and reckless with his place in history'.[33] Blair's position was so weak that he could not afford to fire Short, and instead subjected her to an 'intense charm offensive', securing her agreement to stay in government with the assurance that her department would be heavily involved in post-Iraq war reconstruction under an explicit UN mandate.[34] She recalls that

> Blair had me in there, and was negotiating with me. He got Bush to publicly say he supported a roadmap to the establishment of a Palestinian state as a way of keeping me, and he absolutely promised that there would be a UN lead on reconstruction. And I believed his negotiation … but he was just lying to manipulate me.[35]

Short would stay for now, but blood would be shed elsewhere in government. In a cabinet meeting prior to Chirac's announcement of a veto, Robin Cook had raised a series of very pointed questions concerning the rationale for war and the thinness of postwar planning, and had concluded with a 'carefully worded' statement on the necessity of securing a second UN resolution.[36] When it became clear that Blair could not obtain this, Cook told the prime minister that in consequence he could not support the policy of the government and was resigning. Cook found the conversation slightly surreal, stating that Blair seemed

> mystified as to quite how he got into such a hole ... I got the impression that this was a man who was genuinely puzzled as to how he had got into his present dilemma. I suspect he had never expected to find himself ordering British troops into a war without UN backing. The root problem of the last year has been that Tony was so convinced of the case against Saddam that he never doubted the rest of the world would come to see it his way and had therefore left himself no other way out.[37]

The parliamentary rebellion was now coming to the boil. Backbench unease had crystallized around the figure of Chris Smith, a cabinet minister in Blair's first term. Smith was far from a serial rebel, and recalls that 'it grieved me to go against a government that I'd supported and admired'. The stakes were, however, now too high for sentiment: 'I felt with everything I knew and understood that this was the wrong thing to do.'[38] Smith tabled an amendment to the government's motion authorizing military action which simply stated that 'the case for war has not been proven'. Smith says the wording was

> very carefully chosen in order to try and unite everyone who had doubts, including some who would never under any circumstances have contemplated going to war, right the way through to some who, if the weapons inspectors had come up with evidence, would probably have voted for war.[39]

Of course, given the failure to discover WMD in Iraq, the wording of the amendment would later appear not just politically astute but also quite prescient.

Cook had magnanimously agreed to give his resignation address to the House the evening before, rather than immediately prior to, the crucial vote. The same evening he spoke, 17 March, Blair talked with Bush, who was more concerned than ever about the prime minister's political survival. 'I think I can win, but I'm concerned about the margin of victory'. Blair told Bush. 'I don't want to depend on Tory votes.'[40] Indeed, Blair had let it be known that he would consider his position untenable if he failed to carry a majority of his own party in the lobbies. 'You give the country the leadership you think is correct', he reflected, 'and then, you know, the rest is in the lap of the gods'.[41] He made an impassioned speech, judged to be one of his best, in favour of the motion granting authorization for war. Laying out the long and undistinguished history of the Hussein regime and its lack of cooperation with UN weapons inspections, and encompassing the obligatory reference to the 1930s and the dangers of appeasement, Blair finished with a flourish:

> This is the time for this house, not just this government or indeed this prime minister, but for this house to give a lead, to show that we will stand up for what we know to be right, to show that we will confront the tyrannies and dictatorships and terrorists who put our way of life at risk, to show at the moment of decision that we have the courage to do the right thing.[42]

It was a brave and accomplished performance, consistent with Blair's skill as a politician. It was also matched by rather more prosaic efforts to compel loyalty from the parliamentary party: 'every scrap of patronage and pressure was brought to bear to plead with people to be loyal', Clare Short recalls.[43] Chris Smith received reports that backbench MPs who signalled they would vote against the government

> would be called in to see the chief whip, they would be taken aside by close colleagues and friends that they'd known throughout their time in parliament who'd try and dissuade them, and they would almost certainly be brought in to see the prime minister directly himself.[44]

The crucial vote was won 396–217, but the rebellion inside the Labour party of 139 members was a parliamentary record. This number of rebels, Smith recalls, 'surprised all of us'. For Labour Members to go against their government on an issue of historic significance was

> a huge step for people to take. It's probably a lot easier for an ex-cabinet minister to do than for a first term new young Labour MP, who hopes for a ministerial career in due course, who is under intense pressure from the whips, personal pressure from the prime minister. The fact that 130 of them did I think speaks to the scale of the disquiet, and of course, for every one who actually went through the division lobby against the government, there was another one going through the division lobby in favour of the government, but deeply unhappy about what they were doing.[45]

Blair had won the vote and could go to war, but his standing in the party and the country would never recover. Robin Cook and Clare Short, looking back on how Blair had got himself into a position from which he barely escaped with his political life, offered similar analyses.

For Cook:

> [W]hat was propelling the prime minister was a determination that he would be the closest ally to George Bush and they would prove to the United States administration that Britain was their closest ally. His problem was that George Bush's motivation was regime change. It was not disarmament. Tony Blair knew perfectly well what he was doing. His problem was that he could not be honest about that with either the British people or Labour MPs, hence the stress on disarmament.[46]

While for Short:

> [T]he problem confronting Blair was that his party and country were not willing to sign up for immediate military action. There were two strands in the opposition – one largely pacifist and/or anti-American which had opposed action in Kosovo and Afghanistan. The larger grouping, of which I was a member, was well aware of the evil of Saddam's regime, but also of the anger of the Middle East and the suffering of the Palestinian and Iraqi people. We wanted a way forward through the UN, making progress on Palestine first and working for the disarmament and removal of Saddam without all-out war.[47]

Blair and the war

A realist analysis

As with Blair's other wars, a realist analysis can make some progress in understanding his actions. Again, this had two elements – the perception of threat from the target involved, and the imperative of maintaining close ties with a state as powerful as the US.

The security narrative at the heart of Blair's Iraq policy was focused upon the threat of weapons of mass destruction. The case that Iraq was a direct and imminent threat was, as the prime minister discovered, extremely difficult to make in a convincing fashion. Yet the evidence is that Blair did genuinely view the Iraqi weapons programmes as part of a more generalized security problem, with the potential to combine with international terrorism in devastating fashion. Blair, of course, had dealt with the Hussein issue long before President Bush came into office, with British aircraft and cruise missiles taking part in the 1998 Desert Fox operation. During this period Blair had told Paddy Ashdown, the leader of the Liberal Democratic party, about the seriousness with which British intelligence viewed Iraq's WMD programmes: 'I have now seen some of the stuff on this. It really is pretty scary. He [Saddam] is very close to some appalling weapons of mass destruction. I don't understand why the French and others don't understand this.'[48] Then as later, Blair found himself out of step with other European states in choosing to confront the Hussein regime.[49] By 2003 the threat from Iraq remained, as Blair wrote in the foreword to the so-called 'dodgy dossier' discussed above, 'serious and current'. He remained, confirms Britain's then ambassador to the United Nations Sir Jeremy Greenstock,

> convinced in his own mind that Saddam was a problem in himself, and a defier of international law and United Nations resolutions, somebody who would like to build WMD systems, someone who was definitely building missile systems, someone we thought was still experimenting with biological and chemical weapons and, even if sanctions had constrained him and the UN inspectors had constrained him, would become a threat.[50]

As David Manning puts it, 'Tony Blair took Britain to war because he was convinced that the multilateral option was finally exhausted after twelve years, and he believed Iraq under Saddam posed a serious threat that now had to be confronted. It was as simple as that.'[51]

Indeed, for Blair, the terrorist attacks of 11 September 2001 had illustrated a broader danger:

> There is no doubt at all to my mind that the combination of rogue states with weapons of mass destruction and terrorism is the thing we have got to fear. And the truth is it will only take one time for it to happen and then everyone will say, 'My God, why weren't you doing something about that?'[52]

'When 9/11 happened', Blair commented in 2004, 'it should have been a wake-up call to the world. Unfortunately it was only a wake-up call to America – and to us – ... everyone else has just shrugged their shoulders.'[53]

'States which are failed', said Blair at a January 2003 press conference with Bush, 'which repress their people brutally, in which notions of democracy and the rule of law are alien, share the same absence of rational boundaries to their action as the terrorist. Iraq has used weapons of mass destruction ... Just reflect on it and the threat is clear.'[54] The WMD problem, of course, went beyond Iraq. 'You need to see this thing in an overall context in order to see the threat', he said. 'I don't think you can do this unless you start ... you had to start with Iraq because of the United Nations history and all the rest of it.'[55]

'All the rest of it' included, of course, the fact that Iraq was what the Americans were interested in at the present moment. Dealing with diffuse threats in a unipolar world requires, as a practical matter, the engagement of the single superpower. This has the advantage of ensuring that action could in fact be taken to deal with threats, but the disadvantage that the choice of where and when to take that action might be inconvenient or even ill-advised. As Blair told colleagues in 2002, the 'realities' had changed, US attitudes toward Iraq had changed, so 'like it or not, we have to deal with their new priorities'.[56] In a unipolar world, Blair suggested, one has to accommodate oneself to the policies of the superpower: 'If Washington wants to tackle a problem, you've got to see that, make sure it's true, take it seriously and not run away.' The answer to the recurring questions posed by critics of Blair's policy, 'why Iraq and why now?', is that Iraq in 2003 was where action could be taken, given the engagement of the United States, on a specific manifestation of a general security problem. As Peter Stothard put it to Blair: if we are dealing with Saddam Hussein, why not get rid of all the dictators in the world? 'If they [the US] want to get rid of [Zimbabwean dictator Robert] Mugabe, great, let's get rid of Mugabe', was the prime minister's response.[57] 'In the end', Blair said of America, 'they are the only country with the overwhelming fire-power to do this.' It was key to take a 'stand on the issue of weapons of mass destruction, and the place to do it was Iraq because of the history of it'.[58]

From a realist standpoint, then, supporting the United States' Iraq policy offered the potential at least to begin dealing with what Blair saw as a widespread security threat by joining with the only power in the world capable of doing so. By maintaining a reputation as a loyal ally and offering practical assistance, hopefully influence could be bought over the precise shape of current and future policy, and Britain could be reinsured against some future catastrophe when it may require US assistance. The policies of France and Germany, from this realist standpoint, were imprudent both in terms of dealing with the threat and securing the goodwill of the preponderant state in the system. As David Manning, Blair's major foreign policy adviser, puts it: 'At the best of times, Britain's influence on the US is limited. But the only way we exercise that influence is by attaching ourselves firmly to them and avoiding public criticism wherever possible.'[59] The goal would be, as Foreign Office political director Peter Ricketts wrote to Jack Straw, that

> By sharing Bush's broad objective, the Prime Minister can help shape how
> it is defined, and the approach to achieving it. In the process, he can bring
> home to Bush some of the realities that will be less evident from
> Washington. He can help Bush make good decisions by telling him things
> his own machine probably isn't.[60]

Direct evidence that Blair thought in this way is available. Peter
Stothard obtained a document in Blair's handwriting from September
2002 setting out 'six essential points' that should guide the UK
response to the Iraq crisis. They are for the most part quintessentially
realist in their focus on threat, on the necessity for the weaker to
accommodate themselves to the stronger (see especially point four),
and on the need to work within the realm of the possible. As such, they
bear reproduction in full:

1 Saddam Hussein's past aggression, present support for terrorism
   and future ambitions made him a clear threat to his enemies. He was
   not the only threat, but he was a threat nonetheless.
2 The United States and Britain were among his enemies.
3 The people of the United States, still angered by the 11 September
   attacks, still sensing unfinished business from the first Gulf War
   twelve years before, would support a war on Iraq.
4 Gulf War 2 – President George W. Bush vs. Saddam Hussein –
   would happen whatever anyone else said or did.
5 The people of Britain, continental Europe and most of the rest of
   the world would not even begin to support a war unless they had a
   say in it through the United Nations.
6 It would be more damaging to long-term peace and security if the
   Americans alone defeated Saddam Hussein than if they had international support to do so.[61]

This is a reasonably coherent position on its face, but it is not the only
analysis of the situation consistent with purely material power and
threat factors. The urgency of the threat perceived by Blair, and the
absolutist view of the policy options, was of course not shared by
colleagues in government, or national leaders in other mid-sized
European powers with security relations with the United States. Nor
was his optimism that an international coalition with United Nations
support could be obtained. Further, from a realist standpoint, arguably
the optimal policy position once Blair had realized Bush's determination to go to war was to free ride. The Americans would then deal with
the threat themselves without Britain incurring the costs, and Blair the

political damage, of joining them – this of course was the option suggested to Blair by his foreign secretary and offered to him by the American president. Whilst a realist cut therefore provides an important baseline for analysis, investigation of Blair's individual perceptions and goals is again necessary to develop a fully realized explanation.

Belief in ability to control events

As we have seen in the previous episodes, Blair's high score on the belief in ability to control events trait leads to a proactive policy orientation rooted in a perceived internal locus of control, and a high sense of efficacy in terms of shaping the course of events. The danger, of course, is a consistent pattern of over-estimation of his personal influence over actors and events, and under-playing the dangers of a particular course of action.[62]

There is evidence that this orientation was influential in the Iraq decisions. The Butler Commission, set up as an independent official inquiry into the veracity of the government's claims on Iraqi WMD, reports that Blair in testimony:

> ... told us that even before the attacks of 11 September 2001, his concern in this area was increasingly causing him to examine more proactive policy options ... The Prime Minister's view was that a stand had to be taken, and a more active policy put in place to prevent the continuing development and proliferation of nuclear, biological, and chemical weapons and technology, in breach of the will of the international community.[63]

As discussed above, Blair believed he could accomplish several difficult tasks in shaping the course of events: convince President Bush to seek UN authorization for an attack; convince public opinion in Britain of the wisdom of such a course of action; and convince parliament, and those with substantial doubts in the cabinet, that an attack was necessary. President Bush did seek an initial UN resolution, which the leader of the House of Commons and former foreign secretary Robin Cook states was 'the only point in the whole saga where it is possible to pinpoint a clear instance where British influence made any difference to US policy on Iraq'.[64]

In the other instances, Blair appears to have over-estimated the degree to which he could influence events. Cook reports being struck on several occasions by Blair's upbeat assessment of the prospects of securing full UN authorization,[65] and when this did not transpire, of Blair being 'mystified' and 'baffled' as to how he had got into such a situation.[66] During January 2003, when it was far from certain that the necessary UN resolutions could be obtained, Blair confided in a cabinet colleague his confidence in the outcome: 'We'll get UN cover under all conceivable circumstances. Trust me, I know my way through this.'[67] This was a degree of confidence not shared by colleagues including the foreign secretary, Jack Straw, who had written to Blair as early as March 2002 to warn that a new UN mandate was 'very unlikely'.[68] Ministers were said to be 'united in their slightly nervous wonderment at his certainty' of a positive outcome,[69] while a senior cabinet minister recalls that 'he has got himself into a situation with no exit strategy. He became subject to forces he could not control.'[70]

Indeed, the critique of Blair's policy floated most often is precisely that he became committed to the US enterprise very early, and assumed that he would be able to secure a favourable environment for war through his own persuasive powers. Sir Jeremy Greenstock confirms that 'he certainly gave a very clear indication to the Americans that he would be with them if they had to use force, and I think that was clear a long way back'.[71] By doing so, he ended up 'arguing himself into a corner', in the words of Coates and Krieger.[72]

Conceptual complexity

Blair's low score on conceptual complexity would be predicted to lead him to frame situations in a black-and-white manner, exhibit a largely undifferentiated view of the political environment, engage in limited information search prior to making decisions, and show a general reluctance to reconsider policies. There is evidence that Blair did indeed operate in this manner during the Iraq decisions. First, Blair defined the Saddam Hussein regime in black-and-white terms: it was 'evil'[73] – these 'are not people like us ... They are not people who obey the normal norms of human behaviour'.[74] The justification for action was 'very simple': weapons of mass destruction. The need for military action was also categorical: 'Iraq must be denied the means to make them.'[75]

Cabinet colleagues felt that Blair did not take sufficient notice of the nuances inherent in the situation, nor the range of views on the matter among members of both the British government and the UN.Security Council. Clare Short felt he showed a distinct 'lack of attention to detail',[76] a position subsequently echoed by Sir Christopher Meyer, the UK ambassador to the US until the eve of the war, who noted that while Blair 'liked the vision thing ... he was wasn't interested in the ballast behind the ideas'.[77] An expert on Iraq within the British government, who advised Blair prior to the war, comments a little pejoratively that 'I was staggered at Blair's … inability to engage with the complexities. For him, it seemed to be highly personal: an evil Saddam versus Blair-Bush. He didn't seem to have a perception of Iraq as a complex country.'[78] Indeed, as we have seen, Blair's decision-making style is to focus upon fundamental principles over policy details, engage in limited information search, and be unreceptive to information which does not accord with his existing beliefs.[79]

This provides some explanation for Blair's handling of intelligence on Iraqi weapons of mass destruction, which the Butler report described as 'sporadic and patchy',[80] but Blair apparently viewed as unequivocal. In his foreword to the government's 'September' dossier on Iraqi WMD, Blair stripped the intelligence of caveats, writing

> [w]hat I believe the assessed intelligence has established beyond doubt is that Saddam has continued to produce chemical and biological weapons, that he continues in his efforts to develop nuclear weapons, and that he has been able to extend the range of his ballistic missile program … I am in no doubt that the threat is serious and current, that he has made progress on WMD, and that he has to be stopped.[81]

The Hutton inquiry investigated the process of putting together this dossier, finding that the prime minister had called for its 'strengthening' on several occasions. Presented with the assertively worded final draft, Blair's close adviser Alastair Campbell reported to the authors that the prime minister found it 'good: but I pointed out to him that he is not exactly a "don't know" on the issue'.[82] The Butler inquiry suggested that the interpretation of the intelligence in this dossier went to the 'outer limits' of what was reasonable.[83] John Morrisson, the deputy chief of defence intelligence, went further than this. 'What really irritated me', he said in October 2004, 'was Blair's relentless use of the word "threat" in a meaningless way.' When Blair's framing of Iraq as a 'serious and current threat' was made public, Morrisson continues, 'I could almost hear the collective raspberry going up around Whitehall'.[84] Robin Cook, who as a member of the cabinet and former foreign secretary was able to request to see the same intelligence as Blair, found it merely 'suggestive' without giving any proof that Saddam had 'usable WMD in any meaningful sense'.[85]

Blair's absolutist framing of the alliance with the US is also consistent with a lower complexity information processing style. Robin Cook states that it is a 'fixed pole' of Blair's worldview, not just that the alliance is important (which would not be a particularly distinctive viewpoint), but that the UK 'must be the No.1 ally of the US'.[86] For Blair, there could be no position in relation to the US which stopped short of complete support with commitment of military forces: not for Blair Edward Heath's studied neutrality, nor Harold Wilson's refusal to commit British troops during Vietnam. In Blair's view, any deviation from absolute support in Iraq policy risked the entire alliance, as he indicated in responding to cabinet suggestions that he could perhaps afford to be more critical of the US: 'I will tell you that we must stand close to America. If we don't, we will lose our influence to shape what they do.'[87] Blair, as we have seen, refused Jack Straw's suggestion that on this occasion, given the domestic political difficulties and the lack of international support for war, the UK should qualify its commitment to the US, offering political support but no troops. This was impossible as the US-UK alliance was an all-or-nothing proposition.[88]

Need for power

Blair's higher need for power, as we have seen in the other episodes, leads him to maintain control over policy decisions and processes, and to take decisions with small groups of hand-picked advisers or bilaterally with senior ministers. In the period leading up to the Iraq war, Blair's foreign secretary, Jack Straw, found it difficult to exercise much authority in foreign policy given Blair's close involvement.[89] Clare Short wrote that the Foreign Office was 'completely sidelined, with Tony Blair taking all power to himself and his entourage in Downing Street, and Jack Straw doing his bidding'.[90] Straw confirmed this, albeit diplomatically, by noting that 'There is a recognition that if there is an international crisis on this scale the head of the government will be leading the national effort, and he had sure better be'.[91]

During the Iraq decisions, Blair largely made policy through what has been called his 'inner-inner' circle of personal advisers.[92] A senior minister observed that Blair was wary of open debate: 'Tony says he does discuss this with colleagues, but he does not like things to get out of control', preferring instead bilateral meetings with senior colleagues or making policy in small, informal groups, often on the Number 10 sofa.[93] Clare Short, upset at being excluded from the core policy-making group, reported to the House of Commons Foreign Affairs Committee that policy was made by Blair and his hand-picked, non-ministerial advisers: 'That close entourage … That was the team, they were the ones who moved together all the time. They attended the daily 'war Cabinet'. That was the in group, that was the group that was in charge of policy'.[94] 'Tony Blair and his entourage', Short later wrote, 'were running the whole policy in a very informal and personal way and wanted to keep knowledge to themselves in order to keep control.'[95]

In theory, Iraq decisions should have been taken through a combination of the Cabinet Committee on Overseas Policy and Defence (OPD), a smaller group suited to handling details, and the full cabinet, which should have set the basic parameters of policy. However, Blair disliked the OPD, finding it 'too formal' and 'insufficiently focused'.[96] Consequently, OPD never met, with Blair instead operating through his informal inner-circle. The minutes of the crucial meeting from July 2002 – an account of which opened this book – show that the inner-circle was far ahead of the full cabinet in terms of war planning. The minutes recount that, given US attitudes, 'military action was now seen as inevitable', and 'we should work on the assumption that the UK would take part in any military action'.[97] However, as late as August 2002 Blair was resisting requests from cabinet ministers for a full discussion of Iraq, on the basis that 'Anglo-US decisions are still a long way off'.[98]

Peter Stothard, who spent thirty days shadowing Blair in the run up to the war, found him constantly surrounded by a hand-picked 'team' with whom many of the most significant decisions were made. He also found that members of the 'team' were similar to Blair in policy outlook and work habits, further narrowing the circle of intimates.[99] Indeed, Blair's distrust of the Foreign Office as an institution continued in this period, and he again preferred to conduct foreign policy through a personalized network of advisers reporting directly to 10 Downing Street.[100] In this light, it is significant that Sir Christopher Meyer, British ambassador to the United States during the Iraq crisis, would later reveal that he 'rarely bothered with the Foreign Office' during his time in Washington, instead talking directly to Blair or to his senior foreign policy aide Sir David Manning.[101] Meyer claims that 'between 9/11 and the day I retired at the end of February [2003] I never had a serious conversation on the phone with the F[oreign) O[ffice]'.[102]

The consequences of this style of operation were that when cabinet met to discuss Iraq policy, the formal processes of preparing briefing and options papers and circulating them beforehand were rarely followed. Additionally, most key decisions had been effectively taken by Blair and the inner-circle in earlier meetings. Consequently, cabinet was presented with a verbal presentation of the situation by the prime minister or foreign secretary, in the context of there being a clear 'pre-packed' decision for their approval, rather than an opening to a discussion. As the Butler report states:

> Without papers circulated in advance, it remains possible but is obviously much more difficult for members of the Cabinet outside the small circle directly involved to bring their political judgment and experience to bear on the major decisions for which the Cabinet as a whole must carry responsibility ... We are concerned that the informality and circumscribed character of the government's procedures which we saw in the context of policy-making towards Iraq risks reducing the scope for informed political judgment.[103]

This is perhaps the nub of Clare Short's critique of Iraq decision-making:

> I have made clear, as did the Butler report, that there was not a collective strategy for Iraq and the answer is always given that the Cabinet discussed Iraq twenty-four times ... But there is a great difference between the Cabinet being updated each week on the events they are reading about in the press and any serious discussion of the risks and the political, diplomatic and military options and the hammering out of an agreed strategy to handle the crisis.[104]

Other members of the cabinet saw the streamlined process as less damaging. David Blunkett was piqued by the Butler conclusions, writing that.

> It is decisive action, with proper accountability, that we need, and if getting ministers together quickly and ensuring that we come out of a meeting with a decision is the way to achieve it, then that's the way it should be done. Whether it is sitting around in the Prime Minister's study or whether it is round the Cabinet table is completely irrelevant.[105]

Regardless of the evaluation of their efficacy and propriety, however, there is agreement that Blair ran a streamlined and tightly held policy process.

In this regard, the handling of the legal aspects of the war is also significant. Blair had been asked by Admiral Sir Michael Boyce, the head of the UK armed forces, to secure a definitive opinion on the legality of the use of force absent explicit UN authorization, especially in light of the attorney general Lord Goldsmith's previously expressed view that regime change could not form the core of a legal justification.[106] This Blair sought from Goldsmith who submitted a personal memo to the Prime Minister on 7 March. In it, Goldsmith argued that while a 'reasonable' argument could be made that action would be legal, there were no guarantees that opponents of the action would not bring a legal case asserting the opposite in international courts, and in those circumstances '[w]e cannot guarantee that they would not succeed'.[107]

Goldsmith's opinion was filled with caveats and comprised thirteen single-spaced pages of close legal reasoning. However, when the cabinet came to consider the legal aspects on 17 March, this document was not made available to them. Instead, they were presented with the attorney general's one-page summary of his advice in the form of an answer to a parliamentary question.[107] This had been stripped of the caveats in the original opinion, and did not provide an account of the previous advice nor an explanation for the evolution of the attorney's view. The legal argument was essentially that resolution 1441 had 'revived' the authority to use force in resolutions 678 and 687 – the response to the invasion of Kuwait and the ceasefire in the first Gulf war. Phillipe Sands, author of an exhaustive account of the modern laws of war, suggests that this line of reasoning could 'at a pinch, win the prize for the most plausible answer to the question: What is the best possible argument to justify the use of force in Iraq in March 2003?', but that, if the use of force is not a foregone conclusion and the situation was assessed solely on its merits, the quality of legal argumentation was 'bad'.[109]

Clare Short suggested that it was solely on the basis of the attorney general's assurances in this regard that she had not resigned on the spot over the decision. Her diary records that 'I tried to start discussion and asked why it [the legal opinion] was so late, had he had doubts? ... His advice was that it was legal under [UN resolution] 1441 and that was it'.[110] Short further recalled that

> When Goldsmith presented his findings to the cabinet that day, he began to read out his statement, only to be interrupted by Blair, who insisted that ministers could read it for themselves later. When attempts were made to question Goldsmith, Blair declared that there was no time for a discussion and that the legal opinion was 'clear'.[111]

Blair later justified these procedures by arguing that the attorney general had been present at cabinet, and had presented his full opinion orally.[112] However, in light of the Butler conclusions, this seems a further instance of an informal and highly centralized style of decision making which reduced the involvement of regularized structures such as the cabinet.

What difference did Blair make?

We return once again to issues of actor and action dispensability: would other individuals, presented with the set of circumstances that faced Blair, have acted as he did? What difference did his actions make to the overall shape of events?

As regards the first question, the judgment of Blair's colleagues is unequivocal: 'Had anyone else been leader, we would not have fought alongside Bush without a UN mandate', said a senior cabinet minister.[113] Indeed, while there were substantive incentives from a realist alliance maintenance standpoint for joining the Americans, these were, as discussed earlier, indeterminate. Other states with similar incentives opposed the US action, and the international incentives were more than balanced by the domestic risks. Politicians in democracies are not generally in the habit of launching foreign policy actions that imperil their continuance in office. An actor-general account of the incentives for joining the US and the security rationale for dealing with Hussein renders Blair's policy reasonable, but would also be able to explain many other policy stances. Blair's confidence in his ability to line up UN support and shape US policy, his unequivocal image of the Saddamist regime, and his preference for narrow and exclusive processes are key to the policy output of the British state, and these are rooted in Blair's personality rather than the material environment. As Stephens aptly summarizes:

> There were many reasons – the realpolitik of the Anglo-American relationship high on the list – why he might have decided to go to war against Iraq. And, doubtless, matters of strategic interest played a central part. But the moral certainty that prompted Blair to risk everything on the war came from the conviction that the world would be a better place once it was rid of Saddam Hussein. If the Manichean outlook unsettles even some of his close supporters, a willingness to gamble all distinguishes him as a man who is in politics to change things.[114]

In the Iraq case, Blair's distinctive individual traits decisively shaped British policy, satisfying the condition of actor *in*-dispensability.

As with Blair's other wars, we find a more nuanced picture when we consider to what degree Blair was actually able to shape events beyond the British decisions over which he exercised direct control. To assess Blair's efficacy, we have to understand his goals: someone cannot be indicted for failing to prevent something they really didn't try to stop. The occurrence of the war cannot then count as a failure of

Blair's ability to influence events. As he said at the time: 'If George Bush wasn't raising these questions, I'd be raising them myself.'[115] Given our sensitivity to realist variables, that Blair should be an uneven partner in decision making should not come as a complete surprise, as Britain is firmly the junior partner in a spectacularly asymmetrical alliance. As David Blunkett puts it in defending Blair's choices,

> the situation was not one of equal partners. We were talking here about the only major world power at that moment in time … it was inevitable that he [Blair] was going to have to get as close as he could to the president in the United States, but without a substantial hand to play.[116]

However, as we have seen, Blair did attempt to influence the circumstances of the war, pushing for UN authorization and continuing the post 9/11 case he had made for progress on Israel-Palestine as the key to a lasting improvement in the Middle East.[117] On the matter of the UN, there is certainly a correlation between Blair's efforts to push the Bush administration in this direction and the fact that the Americans did obtain one resolution and seek a second. Matthew D'Ancona reports being 'told by people very close to Blair that Bush's undertaking that he would go through the UN was made very early; certainly by mid-September of 2002, and possibly in principle even earlier. I think that Blair really depended on that private assurance.'[118] However, as with the earlier episode of the decision to attack Afghanistan rather than Iraq following 9/11, Blair's requests coincided with the internal advocacy of Colin Powell. Further, public opinion in the US also ran in favour of making the effort to gain UN approval. Clare Short believes it was Powell's influence rather than Blair's that was decisive.[119] Certainly, an upside of the UN route for Bush was that it helped Blair, but it was a decision he had to take in any case in order to maintain the unity of his administration. A senior White House official comments that 'It became a bit of an urban myth that we did not want to go through the UN. We were happy to go to the UN, but we did not want the UN to dictate terms.'[120]

Seeking an initial resolution was in any case a low-cost move for Bush to make, and the impression was never given by the administration that a failure to achieve it would decisively influence the preparations for war. The issue of the second resolution is slightly different. Many in the administration felt 1441 was all that was needed, and so the effort to obtain a further resolution can be seen as, effectively, a favour to Blair. Even Colin Powell notes that 'We didn't think there was a need for a second resolution, and we were quite sure of very serious problems with the French. But the UK needed and very badly wanted a second resolution.' As Bush said to Blair, 'If that's what you need, we will go flat out to try and help you get it'.[121]

However, 'flat out' may overstate the priority given to the effort by the US. The president's announcement that a new resolution would be sought was a touch diffident about its importance: 'Should the UN decide to pass a second resolution, it would be welcomed if it is yet another signal that we're intent upon disarming Saddam Hussein'. In a private meeting with Bush before he made this statement, Blair thought he had secured a much more substantial US commitment to a second resolution. However, the commitment was rolled back by Condeleeza Rice, spokesman Ari Fleischer, and guru Karl Rove while Blair and Bush prepared to announce the results of their discussions. A member of the British delegation recalls that Blair failed to raise an objection: 'All he had to say was – "George, I need this". He didn't. It was an important moment.'[122] French foreign minister Dominique de Villepin confirms that the US didn't exactly move heaven and earth in support of Blair: 'The British proposals lacked credibility and the Americans did not even really support them.'[123]

When faced with a choice between his commitments to his Doctrine of the International Community and his promises to the US, Blair chose the latter. Sir Jeremy Greenstock felt that 'the US were not walking on the territory [Blair] had set out in his Chicago speech about collective international action', and Blair, for all his efforts, was unable to induce them to do so: 'in the end, when the test came and he had to bet his shirt on one horse or another, he bet his shirt on the American horse, and he's got to stand by that.'[124] For this, Blair may have only himself to blame. Scooter Libby, Vice President Cheney's chief of staff, was puzzled by the emotional heat the prime minister invested in securing a second resolution, given that, as Blair had made clear, 'he is going to be with us anyway'.[125]

On the Israel-Palestine question, Blair again failed to induce much movement from the Bush administration, for which, according to senior cabinet colleague David Blunkett he was pushing 'very hard indeed'.[126] The promise to publish the 'road map to peace', given to Blair in the days leading up to war in order to help him domestically, was a low-cost and largely symbolic act, and there is in any case no evidence of Blair exercising direct influence over its publication.[127] The real test was the degree of follow up from the administration and the pressure that would be applied upon the hard-line Ariel Sharon government to make concessions for peace. This did not happen, and the roadmap quickly dropped from debate. Clare Short, who stayed in government partly because the roadmap was announced, felt Bush deceived Blair: 'it was just tokenistic, and was said to manipulate, and Bush did it for Blair, and never meant it, just because Blair told him he needed it.'[128] Naughtie quotes a 'Downing Street intimate' on the political realities of Britain trying to influence US policy toward Israel:

> People speak of the special relationship with the United States. Not only is it misleading as far as Britain is concerned, it misses the truth. There is only one special relationship in Washington. That is with Israel, because it is the only foreign country that can affect domestic politics in America.[129]

Blair's influence over US policy and the circumstances under which the war was fought is therefore less than he would have hoped. Had he maximized his chances of success? The judgment of colleagues is he had not, promising too much too early, and failing to follow the fundamental principle of negotiation – to convince the other side that you will say no and walk away if the terms are not right. This is always a tricky position for the weaker party to maintain and the British policy in regards to the US has for decades been 'never say no, say yes, but'.[130] Sir Christopher Meyer, the British ambassador to the US, felt Blair misplayed his hand in this regard:

> In the middle of May [2002] I had a conversation with a senior contact at the heart of contingency planning for Iraq, who warned me that the 'buts' in our 'yes, but' position were being forgotten. People were hearing what they wanted to hear. By early July I told London that the UK risked being taken for granted. We were getting too little in return for our public support.[131]

Lord Guthrie, Blair's military mentor, agrees with this analysis. 'I think I could criticize Blair by saying "was he really tough enough about this?" In saying we're going to come with you, you're going to be isolated, but we'll come with you, provided we're convinced that you know what you're going to do afterwards.'[132]

Colin Powell noticed a pattern:

> In the end, Blair would always support the president. I found this very surprising. I never really understood why Blair seemed to be in such harmony with Bush. I thought, well, the Brits haven't been attacked on 9/11. How did he reach the point where he sees Saddam as such a threat? Blair would express his concerns, but he would never lie down on the railroad tracks. Jack and I would get him all pumped up about an issue. And he'd be ready to say, 'Look here, George'. But as soon as he saw the president he would lose all his steam.[133]

Clare Short goes further in suggesting that Blair, having failed to secure firm undertakings from Bush, 'committed us anyway and therefore lost any serious leverage with the US government'.[134] He 'just crawled on his belly and jumped into bed with the neocons, very unconditionally'.[135] Blair allowed the impression to be created in the Bush administration, Meyer reports, that 'we had committed ourselves fully to whatever they were going to do, whether we in London thought we had or not. It was in their bloodstream.'[136]

Could Blair have exercised more influence by playing harder to get? This is the realm of counterfactual speculation, but Meyer believes he could:

> If it all went wrong at the UN negotiations, and the US was faced with going to war alone, it seemed to me that Bush might blink. Or, to put it another way: what the British decided to do in such circumstances could be the decisive factor in the White House. It dawned on me that the Americans really needed us by their side if it came to war. 'Scooter' Libby, Cheney's chief of staff, said to me later that we were the only ally that mattered.[137]

Clare Short agrees that had Blair genuinely threatened to withhold UK participation, his leverage would have been great. She reports being told by many UK ambassadors and diplomats around the world that

> Bush needed the UK because US opinion polls showed that the American people would not support war alone. Our military contribution was insignificant. It was our political support that was needed. This gave us leverage and created the possibility of Blair playing a very important role in history.[138]

Unfortunately, though, Blair 'bought in, unconditionally. And I think he probably thought, "these are big figures in American politics, they know what they are doing"... And so the possible benefit Britain could have brought as a bridge with Europe, and a restraint on the neocon extremism never happened.'[139]

General Guthrie, while putting it slightly differently, agrees that Blair probably misplayed his admittedly weak hand: 'I do think there was a time when a window was open when we were quite important to the Americans, to give them some moral support. I think he could have said "we'll come with you BUT ... you must do *this*".' Blair, whom Guthrie generally speaks of very warmly, had not been strong enough: 'he is quite weak about having rows with people. I saw a little bit of this with Clinton, but I think that it was perhaps even more so [in the Iraq decisions].'[140]

Others are less certain. Donald Rumsfeld, of course, had famously stated at the height of the crisis that British troops were inessential to the operation. 'There are workarounds', he had reasoned,[141] and in material terms this was certainly true. Andy Card, Bush's chief of staff, concurs: 'Would we want Britain to be involved? Yes. Did we need them to be involved? We needed them in the world, but we didn't really need them for military victory.'[142] Victor Bulmer-Thomas judges that Blair's potential influence was always negligible regardless of his strategy, 'such was the determination of the neoconservatives in the Bush administration'.[143]

David Blunkett, following this line of analysis, believes Blair played a weak hand as well as could be expected given the difference in power between the US and the UK:

> In life, the person who owns the car and employs the chauffeur tends to decide whether they are going to drop you off at home or at the end of the street. And I think it's just straight power politics. Our support was welcomed, and our friendship valued, and our words listened to, but there was no imperative to actually take them on board.[144]

Although Blair attempted to play the role of 'bridge' with Europe, this was, for Blunkett, impossible given the attitude of other major European powers: 'Jacques Chirac's attitude and behaviour, and for that matter the Germans, made it very difficult.'[145]

Blair also seems to have been unfortunate in that the marginalization of Colin Powell, the member of the administration whose policy views most closely tracked those of the British, continued and in fact accelerated as the Iraq war approached.[146] Power was increasingly concentrated in Donald Rumsfeld's Pentagon and the office of Vice President Dick Cheney. Rumsfeld's British counterpart, Geoff Hoon, was overwhelmed by the force of the defense secretary's personality and found it impossible to establish the sort of easy working relationship Jack Straw enjoyed with Powell. Blunkett wrote at the time that 'Colin Powell needs all the support he can get, because it is clear that Rumsfeld is far too much in charge. He is just overpoweringly confident, and his deputy Paul Wolfowitz is pretty devastating.'[147] Lord Guthrie sympathized with Powell's fate: 'Colin Powell is a good friend of mine, a very nice man. I think he should never have become a politician. I think he was eaten up by Rumsfeld and Cheney.' This was not entirely Powell's fault, as the National Security Council failed to prevent the bureaucratic manoeuvring of the secretary of defense and vice president: 'I think one of the failures of Condi Rice was that she did not keep the show on the road, and therefore she let the State Department go in one direction and the Pentagon go in another, and the Pentagon is a far more powerful organization than the State Department.'[148]

Indeed, the workings of the Pentagon were fatally impenetrable to the British. A Downing Street aide noted with exasperation that 'it was not just us who were trying to find out what was going on' in Rumsfeld's defense department. 'It was the same for the White House!'[149] This was, however, as nothing compared with the difficulties the British encountered with Cheney. Blair, a politician unusually skilled at getting along with important people, found the vice president an impossible nut to crack. 'Cheney is not very clubbable', says a Blair aide, 'and has a very laconic manner, and does not say more than he has to. Blair found him rather sinister.'[150] Unfortunately for Blair, the reverse was far from true, and Cheney and his aides found Blair's multi-lateralist policies to be quaintly misguided and the prime minister himself to be insignificant. 'Oh dear', 'Scooter' Libby would mockingly remark, 'we'd better not do that, or we might upset the prime minister.'[151] This would not have been of major significance had Cheney occupied the restricted ambit customary to the vice presidency, but as we now know, he was a key figure in every stage of the Iraq story.[152]

The cumulative effect was to put Blair in a fantastically challenging spot, the difficulties of which are eloquently expressed by Chris Smith, the reluctant leader of the parliamentary rebellion. When a common defence of Blair – that really one either got involved in a positive way or else shouted from the sidelines – was put to Smith, he disagreed with the analysis: 'America is a hugely important ally of the UK, but there are times when the role of a candid friend is to say "I'm sorry, but I don't think you're right on this one", and that is what we should have said at the time.' But would it have made a difference to the outcome if Blair had said this? 'I suspect they probably would not have listened', Smith conceded.[153]

Notes

1 J. Kampfner, *Blair's Wars* (London: Free Press, 2004), p. 152.
2 J. Clark, 'Most Labour backbenchers oppose attack on Iraq', *The Sunday Times*, 24 February 2002.
3 MORI, 'Blair losing public support on Iraq', 21 January 2003, www.mori.com/polls/2003/iraq.shtml, accessed 23 January 2006 and

'Iraq, the last pre-war polls', 21 March 2003, www.mori.com/mrr/ 2003/c030321.shtml, accessed 23 January 2006.

4   P. Webster, 'Invasion of Iraq is not imminent, says Blair', *The Times*, 26 July 2002.

5   P. Webster and James Bone, 'Saddam must be stopped, Cabinet agrees', *The Times*, 24 September 2002, p. 1.

6   D. Coates and J. Krieger, *Blair's War* (Cambridge: Polity, 2004), p. 51.

7   C. Short, *New Labour: An Honourable Deception?* (London: Simon & Schuster, 2004), p. 129.

8   D. Blunkett, *The Blunkett Tapes: My Life in the Bear Pit* (London: Bloomsbury, 2006), p. 359.

9   Coates and Krieger, *Blair's War*, p. 33.

10 B. Woodward, *Bush at War* (New York: Simon & Schuster, 2002), p. 335.

11 Kampfner, *Blair's Wars*, p. 219.

12 Blunkett, *My Life in the Bear Pit*, p. 413.

13 J. Blitz, 'Labour MPs demand return to UN over any attack on Iraq'. *The Financial Times*, 9 November 2002.

14 T. Baldwin and D. Charter, 'Cabinet united over Iraq war, Blair insists', *The Times*, Thursday 9 January 2003, p. 14.

15 Quoted in T. Ricks, *Fiasco: The American Military Adventure in Iraq* (New York: Penguin, 2006), p. 61.

16 Kampfner, *Blair's Wars*, p. 255.

17 Blunkett, *My Life in the Bear Pit*, p. 444.

18 Author interview with Clare Short, 30 April 2007.

19 D. V. Natta, Jr, 'Bush was set on path to war, memo by British adviser says', *The New York Times*, 27 March 2006.

20 Kampfner, *Blair's Wars*, p. 266.

21 House of Commons Foreign Affairs Committee (2003). 'The Decision to go to War in Iraq: Ninth Report of Session 2002–2003'. London: House of Commons, p. 41, para. 134.

22 R. Cook, *The Point of Departure* (London: Pocket Books, 2004), pp. 308, 314.

23 Kampfner, *Blair's Wars*, p. 303.

24 J. Naughtie, *The Accidental American: Tony Blair and the Presidency* (New York: Public Affairs, 2004), pp. 144, 145.

25 C. Coughlin, *American Ally* (New York: HarperCollins, 2006), p. 287.

26 Author interview with Clare Short, 30 April 2007.

27 Author interview with Sir Jeremy Greenstock, 6 June 2007.

28 Ibid.

29 Quoted in P. Riddell, *The Unfulfilled Prime Minister: Tony Blair's Quest for a Legacy* (London: Politico's, 2006), pp. 142–3.

30 BBC Television, *Blair: The Inside Story* (part two). Airdate: Tuesday 27 February 2007.

31 A. Seldon, *Blair* (London: Free Press, 2004), p. 594.

32 Author interview with David Blunkett, 1 May 2007.

33 M. White, 'Threat of war: short shrift from puzzled colleagues', *The Guardian*, 11 March 2003, p. 4.

34 C. Short, 'How the prime minister deceived us', *New Statesman*, 16: 760, 9 June 2003, p. 19.
35 Author interview with Clare Short, 30 April 2007.
36 Kampfner, *Blair's Wars*, p. 294.
37 Cook, *Point of Departure*, pp. 320, 324.
38 Author interview with Chris Smith, 18 June 2007.
39 Ibid.
40 Seldon, *Blair*, p. 596.
41 Naughtie, *The Accidental American*, p. xiii.
42 Blair speech to the House of Commons, Tuesday 18 March 2003. Available at http://politics.guardian.co.uk/iraq/story/0,,916790,00. html, accessed 2 April 2007.
43 Author interview with Clare Short, 30 April 2007.
44 Author interview with Chris Smith, 18 June 2007.
45 Ibid.
46 Coughlin, *American Ally*, p. 296.
47 Short, 'How the prime minister deceived us'.
48 P. Ashdown, *The Ashdown Diaries* (London: Allen Lane, 2001), p. 127.
49 Coates and Krieger, *Blair's War*, p. 15.
50 Author interview with Sir Jeremy Greenstock, 6 June 2007.
51 A. Seldon, *Blair Unbound* (New York: Simon & Schuster, 2007), p. 168.
52 P. Stephens, *Tony Blair: The Making of a World Leader* (New York: Viking, 2004), p. 248.
53 Naughtie, *The Accidental American*, p. 193.
54 Coates and Krieger, *Blair's War*, p. 58.
55 Stephens, *Tony Blair*, p. 248.
56 Kampfner, *Blair's War*, p. 164.
57 P. Stothard, *Thirty Days: A Month at the Heart of Blair's War* (London: HarperCollins, 2003), p. 206.
58 Naughtie, *The Accidental American*, p. 2.
59 Danchev, 'I'm with you: Tony Blair and the obligations of alliance: Anglo-American relations in historical perspective', in L. C. Gardner and M. B. Young (eds), *Iraq and the Lessons of Vietnam* (New York: The New Press, 2007), p. 54.
60 Peter Ricketts letter to Jack Straw, 22 March 2002. Available at http://www.downingstreetmemo.com/memos.html, accessed 2 February 2007.
61 Stothard, *Thirty Days*, p. 87.
62 The following sections draw upon my article 'Personality and foreign policy: Tony Blair's Iraq decisions', *Foreign Policy Analysis*, 2:1 (2006), 289–306.
63 Report of a Committee of Privy Councillors, Chairman: The Rt. Hon The Lord Butler of Brockwell. *Review of Intelligence on Weapons of Mass Destruction*. London: House of Commons, 2004, p. 105, para 426 (henceforth: Butler, 'Review of Intelligence').
64 Cook, *Point of Departure*, p. 205.
65 Ibid., pp. 308, 309, 314.
66 Ibid., pp. 320, 324.

67 Kampfner, *Blair's Wars*, p. 256.
68 Jack Straw to Tony Blair, 'Crawford/Iraq', 25 March 2002. Available at www.downingstreetmemo.com/docs/straw.pdf, accessed 2 February 2007.
69 Stephens, *Tony Blair*, p. 219.
70 Kampfner, *Blair's Wars*, p. 255.
71 Author interview with Sir Jeremy Greenstock, 6 June 2007.
72 Coates and Krieger, *Blair's War*, p. 126.
73 P. Webster, '"Evil" Iraq must face action, says Blair', *The Times*, 1 March 2002.
74 A. Parker, 'Blair warns concerted effort needed to deal with weapons of mass destruction', *The Financial Times*, 4 March 2002.
75 Philip Webster and Allan Hall, 'Blair focus is weapons, not regime', *The Times*, 20 September 2002, p. 14.
76 Short, *An Honourable Deception?*, p. 175.
77 J. Glover and E. MacAskill, 'Interview with Sir Christopher Meyer', *The Guardian*, 5 November 2005. Available at http://politics.guardian.co.uk/iraq/story/0,12956,1635029,00.html, accessed 6 November 2005.
78 Naughtie, *The Accidental American*, p. 62.
79 Ibid., pp. 14, 17; Seldon, *Blair*, pp. 599, 616, 624.
80 Butler, 'Review of Intelligence', p. 67, para. 270.
81 Tony Blair, 'Foreword' to *Iraq's Weapons of Mass Destruction: The Assessment of the British Government* (London: Stationary Office, 2003), p. 3.
82 Report of the Inquiry into the Circumstances Surrounding the Death of Dr David Kelly C.M.G, by Lord Hutton (2004). London: House of Commons, p.133, para 212.
83 Butler, 'Review of Intelligence', p. 82, para. 331.
84 R. N.-Taylor, 'Blair misused intelligence', *The Guardian*, 29 October 2004, p. 12.
85 Quoted in A. Rawnsley, 'Peace and war', *Observer*, 8 April 2007. Available at http://observer.guardian.co.uk/blair/story/0,,2049947,00.html accessed 8 April 2007.
86 Cook, *Point of Departure*, p. 102; Naughtie, *The Accidental American*, p. 129.
87 Seldon, *Blair*, p. 574.
88 Kampfner, *Blair's Wars*, p.168, 203.
89 B. Maddox, 'Straw doctrine ducks the issue of real answers', *The Times*, 26 March 2002.
90 Short, *An Honourable Deception?*, p. 94.
91 R. Beeston and P. Webster, 'Straw denies rift over Blair's role', *The Times*, 6 November 2001.
92 K. Guha, 'Testing times for prime minister's inner circle', *The Financial Times*, 12 March 2003, p. 6 ; Cook, *Point of Departure*, p. 112.
93 M. White, 'Blair refuses ministers cabinet debate on Iraq', *The Guardian*, 16 August 2002, p. 1.

 94 House of Commons Foreign Affairs Committee (2003). The Decision to go to War in Iraq: Ninth Report of Session 2002–2003. London: House of Commons, p. 43, para. 141.
 95 Short, *An Honourable Deception?*, p. 147.
 96 Seldon, *Blair*, p. 580.
 97 Memorandum from Matthew Rycroft to Sir David Manning, *Iraq: Prime Minister's Meeting*, 6/23/2002. Available at www.timesonline.co.uk/ newspaper/0,,176-1593607,00.htm, accessed 2 May 2005.
 98 White, 'Blair refuses ministers'.
 99 Stothard, *Thirty Days*.
100 Kampfner, *Blair's Wars*, p. 266; P. Riddell, *Hug Them Close: Blair, Clinton, Bush and the 'Special relationship'* (London: Politico's, 2003), p. 16.
101 Kampfner, *Blair's Wars*, p. 195.
102 Sir Christopher Meyer, 'Seduced by the glamour of American power', *The Guardian*, 7 November 2005. Available at http://politics.guardian. co.uk/iraq/story/0,12956,1636071,00.html, accessed 7 November 2005.
103 Butler, 'Review of Intelligence', pp. 147–8, paras 610–11.
104 Short, *An Honourable Deception*, p. 150.
105 Blunkett, *My Life in the Bear Pit*, p. 667.
106 P. Sands, *Lawless World: America and the Making and Breaking of Global Rules from FDR's Atlantic Charter to George W. Bush's Illegal War* (New York: Viking, 2005), p. 183.
107 Memorandum from Lord Goldsmith to Tony Blair, 'Iraq: Resolution 1441', 7 March 2003. Available at http://www.guardian.co.uk/Iraq/ Story/0,2763,1473011,00.html, accessed 30 April 2005.
108 Sands, *Lawless World*, p. 200.
109 Ibid., p. 189.
110 Short, *An Honourable Deception?*, p. 186.
111 J. Kampfner, 'War and the law: the inside story', *New Statesman*, 17, 2004, pp. 21–3.
112 BBC News, 25 April 2005. Question Time: Leaders' Special.
113 Stephens, *Tony Blair*, p. 219.
114 Ibid., p. xvii.
115 Naughtie, *The Accidental American*, p. 1.
116 Author interview with David Blunkett, 1 May 2007.
117 P. Williams, *British Foreign Policy Under New Labour* (London: Palgrave Macmillan, 2005), p. 194.
118 *Frontline*, interview with Matthew D'Ancona, 11 March 2003. Available www.pbs.org/wgbh/pages/frontline/shows/blair/interviews/dancona .html, accessed 3 July 2007.
119 Short, *An Honourable Deception?*, p. 155.
120 Coughlin, *American Ally*, p. 240.
121 Ibid., p. 273.
122 Naughtie, *The Accidental American*, p. 3.
123 G. Baker, J. Blitz, J. Dempsey, R. Graham, Q. Peel and M. Turner, 'Blair's mission impossible: the doomed effort to win a second UN resolution', *The Financial Times*, 29 May 2003, p. 17.

124 Author interview with Sir Jeremy Greenstock, 6 June 2007.

125 Coughlin, *American Ally*, p. 251.

126 Author interview with David Blunkett, 1 May 2007.

127 Victor Bulmer-Thomas, 'Blair's foreign policy and its possible successor(s)'. Available at www.chathamhouse.org.uk/files/3381_bpblair1206.pdf.

128 Author interview with Clare Short, 30 April 2007.

129 Naughtie, *The Accidental American*, p. 197.

130 D. Reynolds, 'Rethinking Anglo-American relations', *International Affairs*, 65:1 (1988–89).

131 Meyer, 'Seduced by the glamour of American power'.

132 Author interview with Lord Guthrie, 20 June 2007.

133 Seldon, *Blair Unbound*, p. 102.

134 Short, 'How the prime minister deceived us', p. 50.

135 Author interview with Clare Short, 30 April 2007.

136 Seldon, *Blair*, p. 572.

137 Meyer, 'Seduced by the glamour of American power'.

138 Short, *An Honourable Deception?*, pp. 159–60.

139 Author interview with Clare Short, 30 April 2007.

140 Author interview with Lord Guthrie, 20 June 2007.

141 Quoted in Danchev, 'I'm with you', p. 50.

142 Quoted in Rawnsley, 'Peace and war', 2007.

143 Bulmer-Thomas, 'Blair's foreign policy, p. 2.

144 Author interview with David Blunkett, 1 May 2007.

145 Ibid.

146 Ricks, *Fiasco*, p. 28.

147 Blunkett, *My Life in the Bear Pit*, p. 471.

148 Author interview with Lord Guthrie, 20 June 2007.

149 Coughlin, *American Ally*, p. 161.

150 Ibid, p. 160.

151 Ibid, p. 237.

152 J. Mann, *Rise of the Vulcans: The History of Bush's War Cabinet* (New York: Penguin, 2004), p. 369.

153 Author interview with Chris Smith, 18 June 2007.

7 Postwar Iraq

Tony Blair's foreign policy following the invasion of Iraq continued to display the features of a high perceived degree of influence over events, certainty in the framing of issues, and the use of tightly held decision-making processes, coupled with a determined closeness to the United States. Blair's room for manoeuvre was quite narrow during this late period of his prime ministership – having staked his career on Iraq and involved the British state in a war against the better judgment of much of the domestic political scene, he would have found it very difficult to recant the decision or resile from its consequences: 'A confident public voice is the price war leaders must pay', noted James Naughtie of Blair's situation, 'however quavering it may sound inside his own head.'[1] The dynamics that had emerged in the run up to war – an eager prime minister seeking to rationalize and multilateralise US policy without having a very compelling hand to play – continued into the postwar phase. The extent to which Iraq had damaged Blair's standing in the UK, but conversely had strengthened his core foreign policy convictions, was manifest in the summer 2006 Israel-Hezbollah war.

Postwar Iraq

Having made a very personal decision to invade Iraq, Blair would inevitably be judged on the consequences of the war. The creation of a stable state with emerging democratic elements, and the vindication of the initial threat assessment through the discovery of weapons of mass destruction, could have left Blair in a strong position. Indeed, in the early days of the war, there were strong rumours that a successful conclusion to the conflict and a stable postwar situation would strengthen Blair so much that he could remove Gordon Brown from his position of control over domestic policy, and radically enhance his own authority. In private, this was Gordon Brown's fear.[2] The postwar situation that emerged was, of course, far from this ideal. The initial blow was the failure to find weapons of mass destruction. This was particularly problematic for Blair, given that the legal as well as the rhetorical case for war in the UK had rested on Saddam's possession of these weapons. In May 2003, the BBC defence correspondent Andrew Gilligan aired explosive charges that the government had deliberately overstated – 'sexed up' in the phrase de jour - the intelligence on WMD in the notorious 'dodgy dossier' discussed in the previous chapter. The government responded with emphatic denials and an aggressive campaign to discover Gilligan's source, who turned out to be the scientist and WMD expert Dr David Kelly. Dr Kelly, unused to such scrutiny, committed suicide in the midst of the affair. Blair at the time was in Washington DC receiving the congressional medal of freedom for his loyalty, and was visibly shocked when told of Dr Kelly's death – a poignant illustration of the contrasting reception to Blair's policies on either side of the Atlantic.[3] Indeed, the failure to find weapons of mass destruction would cast a permanent shadow over the Iraq decision.

Of more immediate and practical significance was the steady deterioration into civil war of Iraq. A burgeoning insurgency, focused initially on US-UK troops but widening into a Shia-Sunni conflict, prevented the imposition of stability and the creation of effective institutions. While a UN mandate for the occupation was obtained, giving coalition troops legal status in Iraq, the UN itself was forced to leave the country after a devastating attack on its headquarters, killing the envoy Sergio Vieira de Mello. With no weapons of mass destruction and little progress on reconstruction, Blair was in an extremely vulnerable position. Although UK troops, concentrated in the Southern port city of Basra, maintained a general level of order and were subject to fewer insurgent attacks than their American counterparts, the overall difficulties of the occupation eventually spilled over into the British zone. Sir Jeremy Greenstock, the UK envoy to Iraq, warned London with increasing urgency that any good work done in Basra would be undone if the rest of the country became 'poisonous'.[4] Indeed, US forces seemed unable to establish law and order, especially in the capital Baghdad, and many judged that key mistakes were made in the disbandment of the Iraqi army and the aggressive tactics of occupying forces. With his personal authority and credibility fatally damaged and the increasing acceptance amongst the public of the view that the war had been a mistake, Blair announced in February 2007 that all UK troops would leave Iraq by the end of 2008, and that he himself would leave office in June 2007.[5]

Several pathologies afflicted the US-UK occupation, and have been extensively documented in several excellent works.[6] First, the planning for the postwar appears to have been shoddy and based upon highly questionable assumptions. The starting point seems to have been that the occupation would be short and easy, and this attitude was summed up in pithy fashion in a prewar *Washington Post* op-ed piece by Ken Adelman, the Republican who was henceforth known as 'Cakewalk Ken':

> I believe demolishing Hussein's military power and liberating Iraq would be a cakewalk. Let me give simple, responsible reasons: 1. It was a cakewalk last time; 2. They've become much weaker; 3. We've become much stronger; and 4. Now we're playing for keeps.[7]

Dissenting voices were quickly quashed in favour of rosy scenarios, with the Pentagon prevailing in the 'ruthless infighting' within the administration, only to fail to provide a coherent lead having won the battle over the rights to do so.[8] Perhaps the most significant case of this dynamic came when General Shinseki, the army chief of staff, suggested in congressional testimony in February 2003 that 'several hundred thousand' US troops would be necessary to secure post-Hussein Iraq. Paul Wolfowitz, the deputy secretary of defense, immediately termed these numbers 'outlandish', and offered the counter-prediction that US troop numbers in Iraq would be down to around 30,000 by December 2003. This would be possible as postwar Iraq would not be an especially violent place: 'There has been none of the record in Iraq of ethnic militias fighting one another that produced so much bloodshed and permanent scars in Bosnia. I am reasonably certain that they will greet us as liberators, and that will help us keep [troop] requirements down'.[9] As Ricks notes, this hugely optimistic view of the postwar jarred uncomfortably with the alarmist assumptions simultaneously circulated about the existing regime: WMD threat assessments were 'worst-cased' and postwar challenges were 'best-cased'.[10] This optimistic view fitted nicely into the attempt of Rumsfeld in the defence department to move toward lighter, more 'transformational' modes of war-fighting, which de-emphasized ground troop presence and sought to harness high technology and rapid movement. In the postwar period, it became clear that whatever the lethality of a

small, kinetic and technologically advanced army in conventional operations, the grinding task of securing an occupied country required a
very different posture and, bluntly, many more 'boots on the ground'.
Lord Guthrie, the former head of the British military, was alarmed by
the assumptions underlying the US postwar plan:

> The one thing you know, if you've studied recent history, is that the actual
> conflict is quite easy … In my experience, and I have experiences in the
> Far East and in Asia, in the Middle East in Yemen, and Malaya, and
> Oman, the actual post conflict takes twice as long – at least-if not much,
> much longer, than the actual conflict … For Rumsfeld to think, 'quick,
> fast action, give them a bloody nose, come out and it's all going to be
> alright', seems to me to be the most ignorant attitude.[11]

Paul Bremer claims that immediately before departing for Iraq to head
the Coalition Provisional Authority (CPA) he sent a report to
Rumsfeld suggesting that the US troop presence needed to be tripled.
Rumsfeld never replied.[12] The British, Sir Jeremy Greenstock confirms,
'were very conscious that the American system wasn't aligning the
resources to the task'.[13]

The problems with planning went beyond the issue of troop
numbers and into quite basic aspects of logistics, however. Both
Rumsfeld and Franks – as head of the US 'Central Command' – found
postwar planning tiresome and preferred to concentrate on ensuring
maximum virtuosity in the actual war-fighting phase. At the same time,
Rumsfeld, a masterful bureaucratic in-fighter, insisted that postwar
control would be located in his Pentagon, rather than with the State
Department headed by his long-time antagonist Colin Powell. 'No
one at the top level of the administration', writes George Packer in his
excellent account of America in Iraq, 'was less interested in the future
of Iraq than Donald Rumsfeld. Yet he would demand and receive
control over the postwar.'[14]

The goal, reflected in Rumsfeld's instructions to his office of
policy planning director Douglas Feith, was to get to a point where it
could plausibly be said that the 'mission is over and the troops can
leave'.[15] Planning from state was rejected on the grounds that that
institution was associated with a 'nation-building' mission emblematic
of the Clinton years – and a similar stigma was attached to the advice
of the multilaterally inclined British. The plans that resulted seem in
retrospect more like slogans than a guide to rebuilding a country, a fact
exacerbated by the preference for planning by 'Powerpoint', a device
intended to render complex material into simple form but which does

tend to overstate the linearity of things. Lord Guthrie, coming from a British military tradition schooled in the complexities of post-conflict security, ridiculed the quality of thinking on the US side: 'Rumsfeld, Cheney, and I don't think Condeleeza Rice comes out of this with much credit, thought "let's just go and bash 'em, go away, and make them democratic" ... it's lunacy'.[16]

Indeed, this was a cause of great concern to the British and to Blair, who was encountering the nightmare-esque sensation of seeing a disaster approaching but being able to do little to avoid it. Sir Jeremy Greenstock describes the frustration:

> The Pentagon insisted on running the operation after the war, and they hadn't got the right people in place, they hadn't got the resources in place, they hadn't got an understanding of Iraq, they didn't listen to people who did have an understanding of Iraq, and the president didn't have any of those understandings.[17]

Perhaps most surprising given the stated rationale for the war, little effort seems to have been put into searching and securing the suspected locations of weapons of mass destruction. The third of Bob Woodward's books on the Bush administration contains an account of the officer charged with the WMD portfolio meeting with Pentagon WMD specialists and being presented with a list of 946 sites to secure. Pointing out that very few troops in an already light invading army had been designated for investigating and securing the WMD, the officer asked for guidance as to which were the most significant of the sites – were they ordered from 1–946 by size, confidence in the intelligence, or some other factor? It eventually transpired that the list was in fact not ordered at all, and that many of the sites had been added on only the flimsiest of suspicions and in an ad hoc fashion. The officer should decide for himself if, when, and how to work his way through the list.[18]

The result was that, following a spectacular and audacious conventional military campaign that forced the rapid collapse of the Hussein regime, the US-UK coalition found itself occupying the country with a fairly light troop presence and a lack of detailed plans for what to do next. The first head of the occupation, the retired General Jay Garner, improvised with some energy and operated in a climate that had yet to sour decisively. However, he was hamstrung by disinterest and lack of direction from the Pentagon, and some personal failings of his own. A senior British official who worked closely with Garner found him well intentioned but ineffective: 'The trouble with Jay Garner was that he couldn't impose his personality on a sparsely populated bar, let alone a country.'[19] Larry Diamond, who spent a year in Iraq as an adviser on democratization, writes that Garner was 'ill suited for the job of steering a political transition in Iraq ... [he] appeared disconnected from the Iraqi scene, without the will or the ability to learn quickly on the job'. Diamond quotes a senior American official who worked with Garner as stating that there was no real plan or sense of urgency: 'We did what suited us, on a timetable that suited us, and predicated on the assumption that the Iraqis would be passive. Not only passive, but gratefully, happily passive.'[20] John Sawers, UK special representative in the immediate postwar, wrote in a memo to Number 10 that 'Garner's outfit, ORHA [Office for Reconstruction and Humanitarian Assisstance], is an unbelievable mess. No leadership, no strategy, no co-ordination, no structure, and inaccessible to ordinary Iraqis.' Garner and his team were 'well-meaning, but out of their depth'.[21]

Garner was abruptly replaced after just one month by L. Paul 'Jerry' Bremer. By all accounts, Bremer endured a difficult year where his abrasive management style and lack of strategic direction combined with and perhaps exacerbated a sense of lawlessness in the country given vivid expression by the widespread looting of anything of value from public buildings. Bremer's first decisions were perhaps the most fateful of the entire story. On 14 May 2003 Bremer issued orders disbanding the Iraqi army, which he claimed had 'self-demobilized' in any case,[22] and calling for a deep 'de-Baathification' – the removal and ban of former officials of the ruling party from government and other public service. Garner, who had agreed to stay on for a transitional period, saw the order and began to panic. Disbanding the army would have the practical effect of rendering instantly unemployed hundreds of thousands of young men with military training and ready access to arms. It also ran directly contrary to one of the assumptions upon which the minimal pre-war planning had rested – that the Iraqi army could assume many internal security functions, effectively supple-menting the US army and freeing them from the more arduous and politically delicate tasks of occupation.

In terms of de-Baathification, the top ranks of the party, containing the higher echelons of the former regime, could of course not be permitted to continue in public life, but the middle ranks and below were considered perhaps only nominally Baathist, members of the party by dint of it being a prerequisite for obtaining many jobs in Iraqi society. Removing these individuals would do little to erase the old regime, but would have a devastating practical effect on the operation of Iraqi government and society. Geoff Hoon, the UK defence secretary at the time, confirms that the British did not share Bremer's analysis or support his order: 'I think we probably saw it in a different way. I think we felt that a lot of the Ba'ath people were first and foremost local government people, and first and foremost civil servants – they weren't fanatical supporters of Saddam.'[23]

Garner questioned the wisdom of the moves in vivid terms to Bremer, who refused to reconsider the order on the basis that it had come from Rumsfeld in the Pentagon, and he had stressed it was to be carried out even if it caused 'administrative inconvenience'.[24] Rumsfeld, in turn, suggested that the order could not be debated because it had come not from him but a 'higher authority' – which, true or not, did serve to shut down debate.

Perhaps indicating the fissures within the administration, Bremer later claimed he had been 'gamed' into taking the blame for the orders and subsequent negative consequences by the Pentagon,[25] while Condeleeza Rice and Colin Powell apparently found out about it only from the media.[26] Lord Guthrie, a career military man with decades of counter-insurgency and post-conflict experience, indicates how dumbfounded the British were by the decisions. 'To make the army go home, without pensions, without prospects, without pay, but with their rifles ... I just despair at the crass stupidity of people like Rumsfeld'.[27]

Again, viewed in retrospect, these moves scored the double own-goal of making the occupation and operation of the country more squarely the task of a coalition light on troop numbers, and providing a huge boost to anti-coalition movements by turfing out of official life hundreds of thousands of previously privileged Iraqis, many in possession of arms and military training. A vicious and growing insurgency coalesced at this point, and has dominated the story of postwar Iraq since. The anti-coalition insurgency waged a brutal campaign that inflicted substantial costs directly on the occupying powers, forced the re-dedication of resources from reconstruction projects to basic security operations, forced the coalition to operate in heavy-handed ways that isolated it from the population and produced great animosity, and steadily eroded the fragile veneer of multilateralism the US-UK duo had attempted to construct.

This last was especially significant. During August of 2003 insurgents attacked the offices of the United Nations (killing the envoy Sergio Vieira de Mello), the World Bank, the IMF, and Oxfam, leading to these organizations effectively withdrawing from Iraq by November.

Further, the deteriorating security conditions and lack of US numbers forced other members of the coalition – including Spain, Poland and the Netherlands – to engage in combat operations with forces meant for peacekeeping or humanitarian work. With their original missions impossible to carry out and under massive pressure from domestic populations over a war that had never been popular to begin with, the members of the 'coalition of the willing' became increasingly unwilling to maintain their deployments, leaving the US and the UK effectively alone in Iraq.

The insurgency had a further hugely damaging consequence. It prompted from the United States military a response that was more counter-productive than counter-insurgency, especially in its heavy-handed early stages. Ricks records that, given the strategic confusion in the postwar, army units essentially devised idiosyncratic modes of operation in different parts of Iraq. Whereas some units, such as that led by General David Petraeus in the North, operated a restrained and targeted campaign, others, such as that led by General Ray Odierno's Fourth Infantry Division, simply brought to bear the maximum amount of firepower at any sign of opposition activity, operating on the novel doctrinal basis that 'artillery plays a significant role in counterinsurgency operations'.[28] These tendencies toward heavy-handedness had been of concern to the British from very early in the occupation. Sawers wrote to London on 11 May 2003 that the major US unit occupying Baghdad, the Third Infantry Division, had 'fought a magnificent war', but were unskilled and indiscriminatory as an occupying force. 'Our paras company at the Embassy witnessed a US tank respond to (harmless) Kalashnikov fire into the air from a block of residential flats by firing three tank rounds into the building'.[29] While the US army certainly had overwhelming firepower at its disposal, it was not clear that these tactics aided in quieting the country through winning 'hearts and minds'.

A further element of counter-insurgency operations was the attempt to capture members of the insurgency and obtain actionable intelligence from them. Again, the means of doing this were left largely to commanders on the ground, leading to a wide variation in approach. The aggressive Fourth Infantry, operating in the troubled 'Sunni triangle' around Baghdad, took an uncompromising approach, rounding up large numbers of Iraqis in sweep operations, many of whom would subsequently turn out to have little to do with any anti-US activities. The US troops in charge of detention and interrogation, having wave after wave of captured Iraqis delivered unto them, were quickly overwhelmed. 'We had no effective system of triage – deciding who we needed to keep', Bremer recalls.[30] The individuals collected in these operations were shipped to increasingly overcrowded facilities such as the notorious Saddmist-era prison at Abu Ghraib. There, a combination of individual mendacity and confused leadership up through the chain of command led to hugely damaging and widely documented cases of prisoner abuse.

The insurgency, having isolated the US and the UK and retarded the establishment of even basic security in the nation's capital, began to metastasize into inter-faith violence between Sunni and Shia. The occupying coalition, barely able to protect itself, had little hope of successfully inserting itself into a general civil war. Moves had been made toward the establishment of Iraqi institutions, with a series of elections and referenda creating a constitution and a sovereign govern-ment, but it was unclear that the government would survive for long absent the underwriting of the occupying forces. The creation of an Iraqi army and internal security organs to replace those disbanded in the initial phase of occupation proved extremely difficult and slow, and the steady number of casualties in the absence of much discernible progress sapped sympathy for the war in the British and American populace. The initial rationale for war – eliminating the threat of weapons of mass destruction and creating a free and democratic Iraq – appeared quite thin after years of occupation.

Analysis

While the British were by some distance the next largest force in Iraq behind the Americans, UK troops comprised a small minority of the total number. This brute material fact would determine that the shape of occupation policy would be a matter largely for US decision – when one side is providing 95 per cent of the resources and your contribu-tion comes to only 2–3 per cent, Sir Jeremy Greenstock points out, 'you don't have a big voice in those circumstances'.[31] The British, and Blair in particular, would again be in the position of trying to influence a much more powerful senior ally. This was only intermittently possible, with the by-now familiar problem that decisions were being made in parts of the administration that were not at all sympathetic to the British point of view.

David Blunkett felt that, as in the run-up to the war, the postwar was dominated by Donald Rumseld's Pentagon at the expense of the more amenable State Department of Colin Powell: 'I had good reason to believe that Rumsfeld was exercising almost direct control from the Pentagon where he couldn't possibly have known the circumstances on the ground', Blunkett states.[32] Con Coughlin quotes a senior Foreign Office diplomat agreeing that 'Basically, we had been dealing with the State Department'.

> All our postwar planning had been undertaken with American diplomats. Suddenly, we found we had been working with the wrong part of the American machine ... The only place that was deciding policy on Iraq was the Pentagon, and the one place where we had no influence was the Pentagon.[33]

The assumption within the British government had been that the major elements of the Iraqi state - the middle to lower ranks of the army, police force, and civil service – would be left in place in order to stabilize the country. The decision to attempt a rapid and deep de-Baathification, including sending home hundreds of thousands of trained and armed soldiers, caused great anxiety in the UK. 'From a distance', Blunkett told me, it 'seemed to be happening almost without us having any say in it whatsoever ... whilst our commitment and our troops were welcomed, it was very much being operated from the Pentagon and with a particular view that looks, four years on, quite extraordinary'.[34] Sir Jeremy Greenstock, the former Ambassador to the UN, commented that 'in the days following the victory of 9th April, no one, it seems to me, was instructed to put the security of Iraq first ... there was a vacuum, from the beginning, into which the looters, the saboteurs, the criminals, the insurgents moved very quickly'.[35] Indeed, while Greenstock's predecessor, John Sawers, was concerned about over-reaction to any hint of hostile fire, there was from the beginning a much more relaxed attitude to petty criminality: 'Stories are numerous of US troops sitting on their tanks parked in front of public buildings while looters go about their business behind them.'[36] Blair 'constantly expressed his concerns to the Americans', recalls Greenstock. 'The president did listen to an awful lot coming from the British side, but it didn't get translated into improvements on the ground because the tactical decisions were being made by the American machine under the Pentagon, under Rumsfeld.'[37]

More generally, there was an absence of planning for the postwar situation. As we have seen, Blair, with his high need for power, maintained a tight hold on decision-making processes, which restricted the application of the technical expertise found within cabinet committees and the civil service. Clare Short, in particular, felt that this radically reduced the quality of detailed policy making: Blair 'wasn't experienced enough and didn't consult enough to get the policy right ... the British system is perfectly capable of articulating clearer objectives, but that wasn't done because of the way Blair controlled it'.[38] Blunkett concurs that 'some of us ... were for intervention, but for greater discussion about the aftermath – what would happen after, what is the next step. But I, looking back, didn't push that hard enough'.[39]

A further Blair goal was to secure a strong role for the United Nations in the postwar, and he was able to get Bush's commitment to this. Visiting Blair in Northern Ireland in the immediate aftermath of conflict, the president stated the UN would have a 'vital role' eight times. However, as Seldon notes, 'once Bush was safely back home cocooned with ... Rumsfeld and Cheney, his resolve began to crumble, and the UN was clattered out of the major role Blair had envisaged'.[40] The UN did vote on 22 May 2003 to lift sanctions on Iraq and appoint a special representative. But the Americans were unimpressed, Bremer saying that he wanted 'our coalition, not the United Nations – with its murky political agendas – to take the lead in pushing this process forward'. When Sergio de Mello arrived on 2 June and announced his office was up and running, Bremer's reaction was 'Damn. I didn't think the UN would get its act together so quickly'.[41] Indeed, Blair apparently made representations to Bremer urging him to turn over control to an Iraqi government as soon as possible and not formalize the US-UK occupation – advice that Bremer, and his supervisors in the Untied States, failed to heed.[42]

Blair did not waver in his support of the United States and commitment to the policy, continuing, as would be expected of a lower complexity individual, to frame events in Iraq in his characteristic stark terms. The idea of splitting from the United States and withdrawing from Iraq once the difficulties became clear was anathema, and Blair dismissed 'this idea that at the time of maximum difficulty you start messing around with your main ally'.[43] 'Only a complete fool', he declared, 'would not rejoice at the fact that we are the key partner of the world's only superpower.'[44]

Blair also displayed the certainty and clarity of view characteristic of leaders lower in conceptual complexity. In the months after the war, there was 'no doubt' that weapons of mass destruction would be found: 'I'm afraid in that regard, for me the jury is not out.'[45] 'That was the clear intelligence and I think our intelligence people would still say they believe that to be right.'[46] There was also no question of reconsidering the basic premises of the policy in light of the failure to find WMD: 'I do not in any way accept that there was any deception of anyone. I will not apologize for the conflict. I believe it was right then, is right now, and essential for the wider security of the region and the world.'[47]

Blair increasingly viewed the conflict in Iraq as part of the wider war on terror, again mirroring the framing adopted by the Bush administration. This clear cut framing essentially suggested that even if one felt the original decisions were misconceived, there could be no question of retreat from the postwar situation:

> Whatever the disagreements about the first conflict in Iraq to remove Saddam, in this conflict now taking place in Iraq, this is the crucible in which the future of this global terrorism will be decided. Either it will succeed and this terrorism will grow, or we will succeed, the Iraqi people will succeed and this global terrorism will be delivered a huge defeat.

The basic policy was not open to reconsideration: 'The moments that are always difficult are when your own forces are killed or when things happen to the Iraqis, the Afghans, when people's lives are lost. But on the politics of it … I have the positions I have, and I see it through.'[48] This was a stark framing of the issues, and some saw it as a little mono-causal, ignoring the unintended consequences of the continuing occupation of Iraq as a spur to terrorism. 'Those who opposed the war', the former cabinet minister Chris Smith recalls, 'were trying to shout from the rooftops that this whole thing is going to make the campaign against terrorism in the world more difficult, not easier.'[49]

Accounts agree, however, that Blair was unhappy at much of what happened in the postwar phase. Sir Jeremy Greenstock, Blair's envoy to Iraq, stated that he was 'tearing his hair out' at what was happening. Blair's concerns were multiple: 'failure to develop an Iraqi police force and other security forces quickly, the failure to get a media operation going for the coalition, the failure to get other things going more quickly on the ground in Iraq.'[50] Lord Guthrie comments that Blair was 'very, very unhappy' with the management of the postwar situation.[51] The shock of Abu Ghraib and Guantanamo seemed to have affected him deeply. When asked whether he agreed with the view of some in the Bush administration that the Geneva Conventions didn't apply in the current climate, he snapped 'of course not'.[52] In a wider sense, Blair's conception of the war on terror was no less absolute than Bush's, but encompassed a wider range of policy instruments and a more holistic view of the problem: 'If there is a weakness in our current approach', Blair stated in a coded reference to the Bush administration policies,

> it is that in my view you cannot deal with terrorism as simply a security issue. You have to deal with the more compassionate side of the issue – the suffering of people as a result of the Israeli-Palestinian issue, the poverty, the lack of interfaith understanding. All these things need to be part of the agenda as well.[53]

Israel-Hezbollah war

Blair continued in this later period to focus upon the wider Middle East, and the resolution of the Israel-Palestine dispute as key to wider regional stability. In late 2004, following the death of Palestinian leader Yasser Arafat, Blair perceived that an opening for progress existed, given that the Bush administration had effectively refused to engage with Arafat.[54] 'The need to revitalize the Middle East peace process', Blair asserted at a press conference with Bush, 'is the most pressing political challenge in our world today.'[55] The by-now familiar dynamic played out, with President Bush noting that 'I agree with him that it is a very important part of a peaceful world', but ultimately no new initiative was forthcoming. Blair's hopes for progress in this area received further setbacks with the departure of secretary of state Colin Powell, perceived by the British as the most pro-settlement member of the administration, and the failure to achieve much of significance at Blair's March 2005 conference on the Middle East, attended by representatives from the US, Europe, China, Russia and the Arab world, but not Israel.[56] Indeed, on the one occasion when substantial progress was made – the August/September 2005 withdrawal of Israeli forces from the Gaza Strip – Blair was barely kept informed by the US. 'We weren't negotiating with the British government, we were negotiating with the Israelis', said Elliott Abrams, the key US figure on the issue, when asked why Blair had not been involved in the talks. The prime minister was viewed as merely one of many interested parties: 'We kept European and Arab governments informed, but it was not play-by-play information.'[57] Blair was said to be 'angered' by this, but refused to make his disappointment public.[58]

The immediate potential for a fuller settlement was completely derailed, however, by the summer 2006 Israel-Hezbollah war. The war spiralled from a raid on an Israeli border post by the terrorist group

Hezbollah, operating out of Southern Lebanon. This raid successfully captured two Israeli soldiers, creating a hostage crisis as the Israeli government demanded their return. When Hezbollah did not comply, Israel launched punitive air strikes against Hezbollah targets, which rapidly spread to targeting the infrastructure of Lebanon itself, on the rationale of denying resupply to Hezbollah. The assumption on the Israeli side was that the air force could devastate Hezbollah and compel the return of the soldiers, but this proved to be a miscalculation, as Hezbollah responded with a steady barrage of rocket attacks on Northern Israel. The Israeli defence forces mobilized and launched an invasion of Southern Lebanon, resulting in severe damage and loss of life but ultimately failing to break the Hezbollah organization.

Blair viewed the crisis from the standpoint of the wider war on terror, adopting a very similar frame to the Bush administration, where Condeleeza Rice termed it the 'birth pangs of a new Middle East'.[59] Many in the UK took the view that a ceasefire must urgently be imposed given the damage being done to the Lebanon and the loss of civilian life. However, the issues involved of terrorism and kidnapping of Israeli soldiers were, to Blair, 'non-negotiable', a stance that caused him to 'haemorrhage' support among cabinet and parliamentary colleagues, upset at his failure to call for an immediate ceasefire and the perceived belief that the Bush administration was allowing Israel to continue the war in order to 'punish' Lebanon.[60] 'He could have done a lot more' to try to achieve an earlier ceasefire, the former cabinet minister Chris Smith judges. 'To put it mildly, George Bush owed him a thing or two after the Iraq war, and I think he could have pushed harder.'[61] Blair responded with characteristic certainty: 'I have many opponents on the subject but complete inner confidence in the analysis of the struggle we face.'[62] Clare Short saw this episode as indicative of the later Blair's great closeness to the US administration's worldview: 'I think Blair, talking about foreign policy and the war on terror, has become more and more neocon in the way he talks. There's been a real shift in the way Britain talks about the situation between Israel-Palestine, the attitude to the attack on Lebanon, has taken on neocon-type language.'[63]

At the heart of the critique of Blair's Lebanon policy was the charge that once again he had positioned himself very close to the Bush administration, but on the wrong side of a policy issue and without securing much in return. This charge was given almost comical resonance by the so-called 'Yo, Blair' episode, which was deeply damaging to the prime minister's domestic credibility. At the G-8

summit in St Petersburg on 18 July, the president and prime minister
were captured by an open microphone having a private conversation
concerning the on-going Israel-Lebanon war. The president's familiar
greeting to Blair of 'Yo!' was followed by an earthy dismissal of the
efforts of UN secretary general Kofi Annan to end the conflict: 'His
attitude is basically ceasefire and everything else happens. What they
need to do is get Syria to get Hezbollah to stop doing this shit and it's
over.' Instead, the president stated, secretary of state Condeleeza Rice
would visit the region. Blair's response was revealing in terms of his
determination to be involved and, some perceived, slightly subservient
attitude to US foreign policy. Blair suggested he himself could visit 'if
she needs the ground prepared as it were ... because if she goes out
she's got to succeed ... whereas I can go out and just talk'.[64] Ironically
enough, immediately after the prime minister left office in June 2007
he was appointed by the 'Quartet' (US, EU, Russia and China), apparently at the instigation of the US, as their envoy to the Palestinian
authority.

Conclusion

The decision to join the United States in Iraq was the key to Blair's ten
years in office, and in this later period Blair faced its consequences. The
years since the invasion of Iraq have been very difficult for the US-UK
alliance, and for Blair politically and personally. As his military confi-
dant Lord Guthrie notes, Blair 'is an Atlanticist like so many of us here.
We love America, we are grateful to America, and we want to be beside
America, but God, America makes it difficult for us sometimes.'[65]
However, as his prime ministership ended, Blair himself showed little
sign of having fundamentally reconsidered the centrepiece of his
foreign policy. At his last joint press conference with George Bush, he
stated that the US-UK relationship would continue after he was gone:

> I believe we will remain staunch and steadfast allies against terrorism in
> Iraq, and in Afghanistan. The harder they fight, the more determined we
> must be to strike back. I believe the relationship between the US and the
> Britain is a relationship in the interest of our two countries and in the
> interest of peace and stability over the wider world. Sometimes it is a
> controversial relationship – at least over in my country – but I have never
> doubted its importance and I never doubted it is based on shared princi-
> ples and values. I am proud of the relationship we have had, I am proud
> of the alliance of the two countries. I would create the same alliance
> again.[66]

Notes

1 J. Naughtie, *The Accidental American: Tony Blair and the Presidency* (New York: Public Affairs, 2004), p. 150.
2 Author interview with Clare Short, 30 April 2007.
3 Naughtie, *The Accidental American*, p. 16.
4 Author interview with Sir Jeremy Greenstock, 6 June 2007.
5 R. N.-Taylor, 'Iraq: the British endgame', *The Guardian*, 21 February 2007, p. 1
6 G. Packer, *The Assassin's Gate* (New York: Farrar, Strauss & Giroux, 2005); T. Ricks, *Fiasco: The American Military Adventure in Iraq* (New York: Penguin, 2006); Bob Woodward, *State of Denial: Bush at War, Part III* (New York: Simon & Schuster, 2006).
7 Quoted in Ricks, *Fiasco*, p. 36.
8 L. Diamond, *Squandered Victory: The American Occupation and the Bungled Effort to Bring Victory to Iraq* (New York: Times Books, 2005) p. 29.
9 Ricks, *Fiasco*, p. 97.
10 Ricks, *Fiasco*, p. 58-59.
11 Author interview with Lord Guthrie, 20 June 2007.
12 L. P. Bremer, *My Year in Iraq: The Struggle to Build a Future of Hope* (New York: Simon & Schuster, 2006) p. 10.
13 Author interview with Sir Jeremy Greenstock, 6 June 2007.
14 Packer, *The Assassin's Gate*, p. 42.
15 Woodward, *State of Denial*, p. 91.
16 Interview with Lord Guthrie, 20 June 2007.
17 Interview with Sir Jeremy Greenstock, 6 June 2007.
18 Woodward, *State of Denial*, pp. 92–6.
19 Naughtie, *The Accidental American*, p. 187.
20 Diamond, *Squandered Victory*, pp. 35–6.
21 M. Gordon and B. Trainer, *Cobra II: The Inside Story of the Invasion and Occupation of Iraq* (New York: Pantheon, 2006), p. 574.
22 Bremer, *My Year in Iraq*, p. 14.
23 P. Wintour, 'Hoon admits fatal errors in planning for postwar Iraq', *The Guardian*, 2 May 2007. Available at www.guardian.co.uk/Iraq/Story/0,,2070256,00.html, accessed 9 June 2007.
24 Bremer, *My Year in Iraq*, p. 39.
25 Bremer, *My Year in Iraq*, p. 235.
26 *Frontline*, interview with Michael Gordon. Available at www.pbs.org/wgbh/pages/frontline/yeariniraq/interviews/gordon.html, accessed 13 June 2007.
27 Interview with Lord Guthrie, 20 June 2007.
28 Ricks, *Fiasco*, p. 234.
29 Gordon and Trainor, *Cobra II*, p. 575.
30 *Frontline*, interview with L. Paul Bremer. Available at www.pbs.org/wgbh/pages/frontline/yeariniraq/interviews/bremer.html, accessed 12 June 2007.
31 Author interview with Sir Jeremy Greenstock, 6 June 2007.

32 Author interview with David Blunkett, 1 May 2007.
33 C. Coughlin, *American Ally* (New York: HarperCollins, 2006), p. 317, 325.
34 Author interview with David Blunkett, 1 May 2007.
35 BBC Television, *Blair: The Inside Story* (part two). Airdate: Tuesday 27 February 2007.
36 Gordon and Trainor, *Cobra II*, p. 575.
37 Author interview with Sir Jeremy Greenstock, 6 June 2007.
38 Author interview with Clare Short, 30 April 2007.
39 Author interview with David Blunkett, 1 May 2007.
40 A. Seldon, *Blair* (London: Free Press, 2004), p. 621.
41 Bremer, *My Year in Iraq*, p. 82.
42 Diamond, *Squandered Victory*, p. 25.
43 J. Blitz, 'Blair refuses to distance himself from Bush at the end of wretched week in Iraq', *Financial Times*, 15 May 2004, p. 4.
44 Naughtie, *The Accidental American*, p. 203.
45 P. Wintour, 'Blair's evidence to Commons Committee puts emphasis on finding WMD programmes, not weapons', *The Guardian*, 9 July 2003, p. 10.
46 Naughtie, *The Accidental American*, p. 169.
47 M. White, 'It was wrong, I wasn't, Blair insists', *The Guardian*, 14 October 2004, p. 11.
48 Naughtie, *The Accidental American*, p. xv.
49 Author interview with Chris Smith, 18 June 2007.
50 Author interview with Sir Jeremy Greenstock, 6 June 2007.
51 Author interview with Lord Guthrie, 20 June 2007.
52 Naughtie, *The Accidental American*, p. 204.
53 Ibid., p. 202.
54 C. Adams, 'Transatlantic bridge is a bit one way', *The Financial Times*, 12 November 2004, p. 4.
55 G. Dinmore, 'Bush offers Blair no new moves on Middle East peace', *The Financial Times*, 5 November 2004, p. 8.
56 E. MacAskill and J. Freedland, 'Blair hails ripple of change in Middle East', *The Guardian*, 2 March 2005 p. 1.
57 Couglin, *American Ally*, p. 351.
58 R. Winnett, 'Memo reveals Blair's clash with Bush', *The Times*, 27 November 2005. Available at www.timesonline.co.uk/tol/news/uk/article597146.ece, accessed 4 June 2007.
59 F. Biedermann, S. Devi, G. Dinmore and D. Dombey, 'Israel set to invade Lebanon', *The Financial Times*, 22 July 2006, p. 1.
60 C. Adams, 'Cabinet uneasy as Blair fails to sway Bush', *The Financial Times*, 26 July 2006, p. 2.
61 Author interview with Chris Smith, 18 June 2007.
62 J. Ealsham, 'Blair attacks anti-American settlement', *The Financial Times*, 31 July 2006, p. 2
63 Author interview with Clare Short, 30 April 2007.
64 F. Biedermann, James Blitz, Neil Buckley, Caroline Daniel, Sharmila Devi, Daniel Dombey, George Parker and Mark Turner, 'Bush queries Lebanon peace plan', *The Financial Times*, 18 July 2006, p. 1.

65 Interview with Lord Guthrie, 20 June 2007.

66 H. Mulholland, 'UK will remain "steadfast" ally, says Blair', *The Guardian*, 17 May 2006. Available at http://politics.guardian.co.uk/foreignaffairs/story/0,,2081773,00.html, accessed 17 May 2007.

8 The Blair balance sheet

Tony Blair's foreign policy has shown great consistency over his ten years in office. Some of what he has done has been rooted in the inescapable features of the international environment: anarchy, the primacy of military power, and the dominance of the United States. Blair has, over each of the episodes examined here, been sensitive to the security interests of the UK and the potential threats to these interests. Moreover, Blair has sought to cleave as closely as possible to the hegemonic power in a unipolar international system. US power, Blair recognized, had to be harnessed in order to halt ethnic cleansing in Kosovo, had to be moderated in response to the 9/11 attacks, and had to be explained, supported, and rationalized once the decision to remove Saddam Hussein had been taken. In accordance with realist teachings about self-reliance and the ultimate irrelevance of international institutions, this multilaterally inclined prime minister found himself in both Kosovo and Iraq taking major actions without United Nations approval, and did not flinch from doing so. Blair's foreign policy is therefore rendered understandable, and not at all unreasonable, from a classical power-politics standpoint.

But just knowing the brute facts of power politics is insufficient in explaining Blair's choices. His style and worldview, rooted in his underlying political psychology, has decisively shaped British foreign policy over a decade-long era. We can consider the features of his style in turn.

Blair's high belief in his ability to influence events has consistently led him towards forward-leaning, proactive foreign policies. Just listing some of the bases of his intervention decisions – Milosevic could be stopped, ground troops should be introduced in Kosovo, the conditions that give rise to terrorism can be eradicated, the US can be brought to engage in a balanced way with the Israel-Palestine dispute, the international community can be held together over Iraq, the intervention will produce a stable democracy – indicates the scope and ambition of his foreign policy worldview. The crucial caveat, of course, is that laudable ambition is just a bad break away from laughable hubris. At key points, Blair took risks and was lucky – primarily in Kosovo. The flip side is he did on other occasions get himself into situations that he could not, in fact, control, and ended up in very bad shape indeed – the key instance here obviously being Iraq.

Overlaying Blair's proactive policy was a decisive framing of events, people, and situations as clear cut and not particularly complex. An essentially dichotomous, black-and-white view of situations sliced through the suggestions of compromise and accommodation in Kosovo, with Blair reminding all involved of the nature of the Milosevic regime. Again, in the period after 9/11, Blair was comfortable with the Bush administration's framing of the situation: this was a war of global scope against an implacably 'evil' enemy, the stakes were total and compromise was not a tenable position. Finally, the framing of the Hussein regime as by its very nature evil, the stripping of WMD intelligence of caveats, and the refusal to consider more nuanced approaches to supporting the US were clear manifestations of the Blair style in Iraq.

The final aspect of the Blair style is more procedural – an impatience with consultation, collective decision processes, and delegation, and a desire to make decisions with a very small group of hand picked advisers and confidants. This was a style that, in foreign affairs terms, became solidified in the Kosovo intervention, with the daily war cabinets conducted in Blair's private study. The clarity and practical 'can do' flavour of these meetings chimed with the other aspects of the Blair style, and his ultimate success in Kosovo reinforced his preference for these procedures. It was no surprise when they were replicated in the period following 9/11 and the run up to the Iraq war, when the preference for tightly held decision-making processes was overlain with an increasingly personalistic direct diplomacy with the Americans. The nature of the Iraq situation was such that Blair's natural preference for restricted decision processes was reinforced by the difficulties in reconciling the early commitment to be with the US with the necessity to secure international and domestic support – the cabinet had to be kept at arms length from private discussions with the Bush administration. The practical effects of this style varied with the situation – in Kosovo, Blair's reliance on a small, trusted inner-circle kept away from him the

counsel of others to consider a compromise, and the success of the
Kosovo policy lay in that resolute stance. In Iraq, the diversity of viewpoint in cabinet, and depth of caution and experience within the
Foreign Office, was also excluded. Whereas in Kosovo Blair's policies
kept from him advice that would have led to a sub-optimal outcome,
he would, in Iraq, have been much better off had he consulted widely
and followed a more cautious course of action.

This, in skeletal terms, has been the argument of the previous
chapters. For ease in drawing together the research, it is presented in
schematic form in Table 8.1.

What is the Blair 'balance sheet'?

It is appropriate in conclusion to briefly put aside the empiricism that
has guided us so far, and try to reach some more normative judgments
about the balance of good and bad in the Blair foreign policy. How
well did he do as a statesman and an advancer of the values he
professed?

The early results were very good, and can be seen as personal
triumphs for Blair as they flowed rather directly from his style as a
political leader. In particular, the commitment to Kosovo, and the
framing of the issue in stark moral terms, served to marginalize more
cautious voices in the UK, and avoided a repetition of the hands-off
policy of the previous conservative government toward the Balkans.
There is also at least circumstantial evidence that Blair's lobbying of
President Clinton to commit to a ground option weighed in the
balance, although there are suggestions the Americans would have
got to this point on their own anyway. It is also difficult to argue with
the results in Sierra Leone, where again Blair took a risky and proactive decision that served to stop vicious thuggery against a civilian
populace.

Blair was, however, fortunate in the early years of his prime ministership to be operating alongside a US ally committed to a liberal inter-
nationalist foreign policy. Blair's own Doctrine of the International
Community was more ambitious than Clinton's foreign policy, but the
two were basically compatible. Blair, in this dyad, was the more aggressive of the two leaders, and he fundamentally understood the instincts
and style of the Clinton White House – his own 'New Labour' had,
after all, taken as its inspiration Clinton's 'New Democrats'.

Table 8.1 *Predictions and evidence from realist and personality variables: summary of the argument*

Variable	Predictions	Evidence from Kosovo & Sierra Leone	Evidence from 9/11 & Afghanistan	Evidence from Iraq
Realism: power and threat	• Focus upon security threats. • Asymmetrical alliance dynamics. • Utility of maintaining close alliance with US.	• Instability in Balkans & from Kosovar refugees could potentially spread & become a wider security problem. • Necessity of harnessing the power of the US in order to stop Milosovic.	• Blair's attempt to forge close relationship with Bush both pre & post 9/11. • Attempt to restrain hegemon from uncontrolled response to attacks. • Focus upon threat from failed states/terrorism nexus.	• Once direction of US policy is clear, Blair accommodates the UK to it. • Sustained focus (from 1998 on Iraq's WMD programmes as threat. • Iraq seen as specific case of rogue state/WMD/terrorist nexus. • British conditions for going to war are regarded as inessential by the US. • Postwar decsions taken by US with little regard for UK views.

continued overleaf

Table 8.1 *Continued*

Variable	Predictions	Evidence from Kosovo & Sierra Leone	Evidence from 9/11 & Afghanistan	Evidence from Iraq
High belief in ability to control events	• Proactive policy stance. • Ambitious goals. • Danger of over-reach.	• Very forward-leaning position on use of force & ground troops. • Promises return of refugees to Kosovo; ties NATO's credibility to achieving this goal. • Belief that he can persuade President Clinton to maintain the bombing & introduce ground troops.	• Huge policy agenda focusing on eradicating not only terrorism, but also the conditions that give rise to it. • Seeks to revitalize Israel-Palestine peace process. • Overestimation of ability to personally influence US policy & rally Middle Eastern support for Afghanistan war.	• Belief can influence US to seek UN approval, build a wide-ranging coalition. • Believed UN approval obtainable. • Judgement that he could persuade parliamentary party & public to support the war. • Continued overestimation of ability to influence US to engage with Israel-Palestine.
Low conceptual complexity	• Black & white view of issues & actors. • Discomfort with policy detail. • Unwillingness to reconsider direction of policies.	• Milosovic an 'evil' & 'barbarous' dictator. • Refusal to consider 'fudge' compromise deal to halt war.	• Manichean framing of 'evil' terrorists, 'civilisation vs barbarism'. • Acceptance of 'war on terror' frame propounded by Bush administration.	• Hussein regime 'evil'. • Intelligence on WMD viewed as more clear-cut than evidence supported. • Alliance with US an all-or-nothing proposition. • Little consideration of alternative policy analyses & options. • Refusal to reconsider commitment to Iraq or basic decisions in light of postwar problems.

continued

Table 8.1 *Continued*

Variable	*Predictions*	*Evidence from Kosovo & Sierra Leone*	*Evidence from 9/11 & Afghanistan*	*Evidence from Iraq*
High need for power	• Decisions made in small groups & bilaterally. • Decisions reflect personal preferences of prime minister rather than collective will of government. • Regular decision-making channels, in particular cabinet & Foreign Office, downplayed or ignored.	• Once issue becomes high profile, Blair takes over Kosovo policy from foreign secretary. • Micromanages air campaign. • Daily war cabinet meets in PM's study. • Frustration with beaurocracy & caution of Foreign Office.	• Personalistic diplomacy, travelling with very small groups of aides. • Policy decisions made in consultation with chief-of-staff & communications director in Downing Street 'den'. • Cabinet meetings devoid of real debate. • Little use of or consultation with Foreign Office. • Increasing reliance on direct consultations with Bush & Condeleeza Rice.	• Iraq policy made through 'inner-inner circle' of advisers. • Cabinet kept only marginally informed, largely acting as a 'rubber stamp' for decisions made elsewhere. • Restricted discussion on under-takings given to US, alternatives to policy, and legal aspects of war. • Regular Foreign Office channels not utilised.

Things began to go badly when a new administration, and the transformative influence on American foreign policy of 9/11, flipped Blair's relationship with the United States: he would now be compelled to restrain rather than stiffen the senior ally. This is a task for which his style – evangelical, Manichean, and directive – is peculiarly ill-suited, and for which the resources at his command – a junior ally with a comparatively insignificant military capacity – were thin. In the post-9/11 period, Blair followed the obvious course of offering strong public support for the US and seeking to ensure that its response would be sensible and well-considered. His style found manifestation in the laudable efforts to build international support for the United States, and to focus attention not just on the manifestations of international terrorism, but the root causes of this type of problem in international affairs.

The Bush administration, however, was less interested in international community and in the root causes of terrorism, and began to direct its energies toward dealing with the old problem of Iraq. From this point on, we must be harsher on Blair. To be sure, he faced an extremely difficult situation in seeking to manage the consequences of America's focus on Iraq, and his policy choices were not irrational nor can we say with confidence that different choices would have produced a better outcome. The basic facts of international life constrained Blair's actual ability to influence events, whatever his individual perception of that ability might have been. The United States is the pre-eminent power in the world, and as a liberal, English-speaking power this is far from the worst situation that the British could face. There is little evidence that the strategy of the French and the Germans served their interests particularly well and it certainly did not weigh at all in the calculations of the Americans.

Further, some of the central critiques of Blair's policy appear more compelling in retrospect than they did at the time. Most obviously, the mismanagement of the postwar by the United States has cast the Iraq decision in a more negative light than he could have expected. Blair, surveying the depth of experience in the Bush administration, must surely be surprised at how poor the postwar strategizing has been. After all, the Bush administration itself derived no obvious benefit from a chaotic post-Saddam Iraq, and the shambolic occupation damaged their reputations as much as Blair's. The prime minister's strategy of getting involved on the side of the US and seeking to influence the manner in which they went about dealing with Iraq certainly had a lot to commend it given the situation at the time, if only because of the absence of realistic alternatives. Nonetheless, at least four key failures in Blair's policy must be addressed.

First, Blair badly misread the bureaucratic politics of the Bush administration. The evidence indicates that Bush and Blair talked regularly and that the president listened to the prime minister. However, as study after study of the Bush White House has noted, the president, inexperienced in foreign affairs, relied heavily upon his advisers in matters of policy. In lobbying the administration, then, Blair's efforts were focused upon the ideologically amenable Colin Powell, with whom foreign secretary Jack Straw had formed a close relationship, and Condeleeza Rice, whom Blair's adviser David Manning spoke with regularly.

However, we now know that Powell in particular was a marginalized and frustrated figure in Iraq decision making, and of course he left the Bush administration after the president's reelection. Rice's role was as a procedural figure rather than advocate, and in the first Bush term she was regularly out-manoeuvred by more experienced and ruthless players of the game. Of these, Blair had far less contact with and influence over Donald Rumsfeld and Dick Cheney – the two members of the administration who shaped Iraq policy and postwar planning. The British were reassured by the presence of Colin Powell without realizing that Rumsfeld and Cheney, who thought about the issues in a very different way, were in fact exercising the real decision-making power. Having adopted the strategy of seeking to influence the Bush administration through getting involved in its internal deliberations, Blair should have ensured he understood what the divisions were and where the balance of power lay.

A related failing involves the prime minister's sketchy understanding of the administration's neoconservative contingent, which increasingly won the battle to define the president's thinking on Iraq. As discussed in Chapter 5, neoconservatism is a well-defined set of principles for thinking about the world that has been elucidated in many documents, both governmental and public, over the past fifteen years. That there were many powerful adherents of its doctrines within the Bush administration was well known. However, there is little evidence that Blair either recognized or gave sufficient weight to this when considering the alliance during this period.

To be sure, there were elements of overlap between Blair's worldview and that of the neoconservatives – in particular a proactive stance in relation to security threats from rogue regimes, and a belief that powerful liberal states can use their military capacity to promote their values. However, as Sir Jeremy Greenstock eloquently put it, the American neoconservatives were 'not walking on the same ground' as paved by Blair's Doctrine of the International Community.[1]

Most obviously, neoconservatives deny the notion of an 'international community' at all, regarding international institutions and coalitions as constraints upon the superpower's freedom of action, and therefore to be viewed with suspicion. Furthermore, neoconservatism has a strong pro-Israel stance, and several neoconservatives have ties to the hawkish Israeli Likud party. Why, the question must be asked, would Blair believe that an administration with neoconservatives in the ascendancy would operate in good faith through the United Nations in dealing with Iraq and would move on a parallel track toward pressuring the Ariel Sharon government to reach an accommodation with the Palestinians? A reading of even a small selection of neoconservative literature would indicate that neither of these conditions is likely to be willingly fulfilled, and certainly not as a favour to a very junior third party.

Indeed, a further critique of Blair's Iraq policy we might level is precisely the timidity with which the conditions for committing to the invasion were held to. The prime minister's negotiating strategy, as the UK ambassador to the US Sir Christopher Meyer in particular has stated, was to commit first and ask for things later – the classic British 'yes, but' stance. However, the basic principle of negotiation is that you must convince the other side that you are ultimately willing to walk away under certain conditions. The impression left on the Bush administration, as I documented in Chapter 6, was that Blair would be with them under all circumstances. For an administration with the single-mindedness of the 2002–03 vintage Bush White House, this all but ensured that minimal compromise would be forthcoming. This is not to say that a more demure attitude would have secured more of what Blair wanted – that is the realm of the unknowable. What we can say is that Blair asked neoconservatives to do things that even a surface-level reading of their worldview suggests they would not readily do, and then failed to specify any negative consequences should they not do them.

Finally, it is clear in retrospect that Blair was too trusting of the Bush administration's competence in and attention to postwar planning. As reported in Chapters 6 and 7, several senior ministers close to Blair, including Jack Straw and David Blunkett, worried that there was little evidence the Americans had fully thought through the postwar. John Sawers, on arrival in Baghdad immediately after the fall of the regime, cabled back with severe reservations about the initial steps taken by the US army and Jay Garner, reservations that continued to be transmitted to London by Sir Jeremy Greenstock during the tenure of the CPA. As it became clear that the occupation was a) going badly and b) being run almost exclusively by the Pentagon, Blair maintained his public support and failed to achieve, whatever concerns were expressed in private, a more effective and coherent coalition policy in Iraq. While the area under direct British control in Basra was managed in accordance with accepted doctrines of post-conflict reconstruction and remained quiet for a time, the instability in the heart of the country inevitably spilled over even there.

What does this mean for International Relations theory?

While answering the questions above has drawn us into the murky waters of counter-factual speculation and normative judgments, we return to more solid ground in briefly considering the implications of the study for IR theory.

In terms of foreign policy analysis, we can reaffirm the fundamental standpoint of that field: actor-specific theory is important because individual choices and decision-making processes exercise significant influence over the foreign policies of states and over broad international outcomes. More specifically, the congruence between the profile of Blair generated by Margaret Hermann's trait analysis technique and his behaviours across a decade in power represent important additional confirmation for the validity of her measurement technique. Given the continuity in Blair's policies across different policy episodes, we can also consider this study as weighing on the side of consistency of personality across situation in the 'state-vs-trait' debate.

However, the study also speaks importantly to more general issues in international relations theory, and acts as a caution against actor-specific reductionism. Whatever Blair's individual characteristics, he would have faced an international situation characterized by threats from rogue regimes, and an inherited alliance with the hegemon in a unipolar international system. Aspects of Blair's choice, as I have repeatedly stressed, were strongly shaped by actor-general features of the circumstances he faced. This is to say that the case of Tony Blair stands in support of the instincts of the neoclassical realist movement that power politics is the best place to begin in analysis of foreign policy, but that environmental factors are indeterminate and are mediated, to a degree crucial for accurate prediction and explanation, by sub-state and ultimately individual-level variables. This study could therefore be a caution to foreign policy analysts to consider how far system-level explanations account for the phenomena they wish to explain, and an invitation to neoclassical realists to engage fully with the tools and concepts of actor-specific theory in order to refine their use of sub-state level variables.

Conclusion

In the end, character is destiny. Blair's successes and failures were those of a leader with a proactive and self-confident nature, who sees the world in clear-cut terms, and who makes choices quickly, decisively, and with little consultation. As Sir Jeremy Greenstock aptly concludes,

> The prime minister has a style which is determined. Once he sets his hand to something, he's going to see it through, and in every previous instance up to Iraq, it worked. But of course, if you take that on, you hit a Peter Principle, where you run out of luck or you hit the ceiling of your competence ... You keep going, and that is an admirable characteristic when it ends up in success, but you are vilified when it ends in failure.[2]

Notes

1 Author interview with Sir Jeremy Greenstock, 6 June 2007.
2 Ibid.

Index